THE
UNDAUNTED
LIFE

THE
UNDAUNTED
LIFE™

How to Succeed No Matter What

Robert C. David

Bob David Live, Inc.
Richmond, Virginia

Published by:
Bob David Live, Inc.
www.BobDavidLive.com

Cover design by George Foster, Foster Covers
Interior design by Dorie McClelland, Spring Book Design

ISBN: 978-0-9825646-0-8

First edition
Printed in the United States of America
15 14 13 12 1 2 3 4

This book is dedicated to my devoted parents for being role models of persistence, hard work, compassion and integrity; to my cherished wife Cheri for being the love of my life and my undaunted life partner; to my beloved son Matthew and daughter Graciella for your bright smiles, spontaneous hugs and unbridled enthusiasm; to my dear family, friends, mentors, coaches, colleagues, business associates and clients for your inspiration, encouragement and ongoing support.

CONTENTS

INTRODUCTION

Undaunted. It's unlikely you've seen this term used very often, but rare times call for rare words. And like discovering a lost treasure chest from a bygone era, this word's meaning contains precious character traits and virtues worth untold riches to those willing to unlock its secrets. What does the word "undaunted" mean? Here's a dictionary definition:

> **Undaunted**: adj. not discouraged, undismayed, unfazed; resolute, courageous, unshrinking, valiant, stalwart, unflinching, stouthearted, heroic, brave, indomitable, fearless, bold, purposeful, determined to succeed.

Please take a moment and read that definition again. . . . Let your mind, body and soul bask in the radiance of its powerful glow. How are you feeling now? Inspired, reassured? If you will but sound the welcome trumpets and lower the drawbridge to your castle, you will see a regal white horse riding in gallantly to be by your side—helping you fight and win your life's many battles. This silent partner delivers a potent message sure to fortify your defenses and help unleash your inner hero when you need it most—to succeed no matter what!

Given everything that's been happening in our world, can you see why we need this word in our vocabulary arsenal now more than ever before? Think about your most pressing life and work challenges. How's your attitude? Your finances? Your health? Your energy level? Your career, business or job satisfaction? How are your personal and professional relationships? How's your overall happiness? Are you performing at your fullest potential? Are you achieving your goals? Do you have a sense of purpose, contribution and accomplishment?

What kind of adversity are you experiencing? What kinds of setbacks, heartbreaks, failures, disappointments or detours have you endured on your journey?

Whatever your answers to these life and work questions, my message to you is "hang in there"—help is on the way! What if you could be shielded from all the negativity and uncertainty that bombards us almost every day? What if you were equipped with the wisdom and clarity that gave you shelter from the storms and winds of change? What if you were armed with the right awareness, mindset and insights that bring peace of mind? What if you developed the right strategies and action steps to move boldly and confidently in the direction of your dreams? What if you became so empowered, so unstoppable that you knew you would succeed no matter what was going on around you? In short: What if YOU became undaunted?

THE NAKED TRUTH

The legendary investor Warren Buffet once said in one of his annual letters to shareholders regarding adversity and business that when the tide rolls out, we're going to see who's been swimming naked. Well, for many individuals and organizations these days, the tide has not only rolled out, it's knocked them off their feet and pulled them out to sea to drown. The economy impacts everyone, but clearly some more than others. It sure helps if you are lucky enough to move your 401k to cash, for example, before a bear market begins. Or if you happen to be a heart surgeon with a recession-proof income stream. But for the majority, when tough times hit, whether related to your work or your personal life, it's a long, arduous swim back to shore.

Some give up hope, turning to the government for answers. Some turn to faith. Some turn to family for a life preserver. And, unfortunately, some turn to crutches for escape: drugs, alcohol, tobacco, food, shopping, sex, gambling, etc. Many abandon hopes for college, retirement, a better job or a second career and simply tread water, hoping for calmer seas. For others, tough times serve as a wake-up call to return to the basics and learn some life lessons.

Whenever tough times hit in business or in life, there are always plenty of gloom-and-doomers out there predicting the worst is yet to come. Many fear that their best days are behind them. They've put their dreams on the shelf. They've lowered their sights, pulled in their oars and drawn in their sails. When we're hit with sub-prime blowups, lingering recessions, Wall Street scandals, record deficit spending, and bear markets in stocks and real estate, our confidence gets shaken to the core. It's pretty chilly when the tide rolls out and we are fully exposed to those bracing, turbulent winds of change.

But despite any of those stormy conditions that may rise up at any time, I want to make you a bold promise. With the right attitude, insights, success strategies and action steps, you can become someone who will never have to worry about the tide again. Because when that tide invariably rolls out, you will not only have on your bathing suit, you'll be looking good in it—wiggling your toes in the sand and wearing a big grin on your face. While others are lost at sea, you'll be surfing the waves of change. You'll enjoy the kind of freedom, peace of mind and abundance you were destined to have—living your life your way on your terms. This is what being undaunted is all about.

WHO'S THAT HERO IN THE MIRROR?

There is a disturbing trend in our country. Many people are increasingly looking for answers from the government and institutions. Why? Wouldn't you agree that the vast majority of resources we need are standing in our own shoes? They are within the person looking back at us in the mirror. It's time for a resurgence of the values of self-reliance and self-determination. Others may be giving up on capitalism, free enterprise and a culture that rewards innovation, risk taking and excellence. But the answers lie in learning how to discover, harness and maximize the unique potential of every individual. And in the process unleash the power that made this country great in the first place—the power of personal responsibility, freedom and liberty.

Yes, there has been no better time to unleash that inner hero, just waiting to be called into action. Instead of seeing ourselves as pawns in the chess game of life, we can remember that we have far more power to make bold moves on our playing board than we realize. We can learn to take command and control in any situation—to succeed and win regardless of the environment or what the competition is doing. And we can all become the kings and queens of our own castles in the process. We really can learn how to succeed no matter what is going on with our economy, our government, our industries, our communities—basically anything beyond our immediate control outside ourselves. This is no time to be timid, no time to surrender! This is a time to take the lead.

Learning to be undaunted doesn't mean we don't have problems. We will always be faced with challenges, obstacles, negativity, difficult people and circumstances that may cause temporary setbacks. Living the undaunted life simply means that we learn how to think, perform and succeed regardless of what's going on in our outer world. We learn to be the masters of our own destinies and in the process maximize our positive impact on others, our society and our world. You can become a true hero if you will but seize the moment.

MAKE HOPE REAL

Have you ever been unemployed, or know someone who is? Have you ever been fired, laid off, downsized, rightsized, realigned, reassigned, outsourced or commoditized? Is your business or career in trouble? Has your net worth recently shrunk because of the changing economy? Have your dreams of retirement been shattered? Do you feel like your life is out of your control? Have your relationships suffered because of the added stresses brought on by outer circumstances? Is your energy level being sapped by the constant drip of bad news in the media? Are you yearning to do what you'd really like to do with your life? Are you seeking your true calling? Do you want to make a real difference in the lives of others? Do you wonder what it would be like to perform to your fullest potential? Do you ever find yourself "de-motivated" at work? Do you find yourself doing more work for less money? Do you ever find yourself wondering if you will ever have any fun again?

If you find yourself answering "yes" to many of these questions, then you are reading the right book. These are just some of the challenges we'll be tackling. It's my goal to not only give you hope but also show you how to make that hope a reality in your life and in your work.

Don't let the outside world determine your destiny. Take control now, with proven success strategies that will help you become richer, smarter, healthier and happier in spite of it all. This book will serve as a fresh, bold guide for your ultimate quest—to bravely and freely live your best life on your own terms. Starting right now. As you read the chapters ahead you will soon discover how to:

- Unlock, harness and nurture your natural talents, strengths and abilities;

- Achieve focus and gain insights to work smarter so you can live better;

- Tap your reservoir of resiliency during tough times and find ways to turn them to your advantage;

- Eliminate financial self-sabotage from your decisions in business and in life;

- Vanquish procrastination and self-limiting thoughts, beliefs and emotions;

- Grow Referral Rich—and forge stronger and deeper relationships to serve you in any business;

- Experience more joy, meaning, purpose and passion in your life.

You will find these strategies applicable to your work in any business or industry. This book will speak to you whether you are an advisor, entrepreneur, an executive, a small business owner, a manager, an employee, or anyone looking to make positive change in your own world.

Why am I writing this book? What have I learned about living the undaunted life that helps me serve as your guide? To fully appreciate the answer to this question, I ask that you indulge me for just a few moments as we go back in time together. We are all shaped by certain life events more than others, often called "defining moments." One of the biggies for me happened back in high school when I was a scrawny ninth-grade saxophone player in the marching band. Like most teens, I lacked focus and discipline. I was floating along aimlessly. But my life was changed forever one day when I was sitting in the bleachers of our gym at a pep rally for our football team.

Picture hundreds of noisy, rowdy teenagers cheering, "We're number one, we're number one!" as the head football coach strolled confidently towards a microphone on a stand at center court. As he took the microphone and began to speak, something extraordinary happened. The crowd suddenly went dead silent. Then, to my amazement, he didn't talk about football at all. Instead, he delivered a motivational message about how to succeed in life! It was so spellbinding and compelling, I immediately committed to setting many new and daunting life goals—one of which was to leave the band and join the football team.

I was about to begin my rite of passage. I'll explain why. The football program was unique in that there were no "cuts." All you had to do to make the team was simply not quit. You see, the practices were so physically demanding and psychologically intimidating that most players left voluntarily. After experiencing many initial failures, setbacks and humiliating defeats on the Junior Varsity squad, I certainly had every reason to quit. Only the encouraging words of the head varsity coach playing over and over in my mind kept me determined to stick it out in the hopes of eventually turning things around.

I decided to focus on the only thing I had absolute control over—my physical body. I embarked on a highly disciplined workout and diet regimen, which, combined with a timely growth spurt, resulted in a complete physical transformation. When I reported for summer practice, coaches and players alike were shocked to see me (and no, I did not use steroids). I had become a new person.

But new muscles alone were not going to get me on the playing field. It took a combination of tenacity, boldness and luck during those intense summer sessions to get my chance. And when it came early in the season that junior year, I took full advantage and ultimately became a starter on offense and defense on a team that went 15–0, won the Georgia AAAA State Championship and earned the number one ranking in the nation by a prominent sportswriters' poll. I was labeled a before-and-after success story and earned the team's Most Improved Player award. A major newspaper article referred to me as "A Self-Made Player." The life lessons learned that season would serve as a foundation for everything I have achieved in business and in life so far.

Having gained confidence from my success on the gridiron, I began speaking to groups my senior year about our storied championship experience. That taught me that one of the best ways to become an expert at something is to teach it. While public speaking was initially very intimidating, I ultimately found myself really enjoying it. I was becoming what I admired most in my mentor. I was learning how to inspire and coach others how to succeed.

I went on to earn a full football scholarship at Furman University and helped our team win three Southern Conference Championships under the leadership of another remarkable coach. Those winning seasons included major upset victories over much larger, better financed schools such as Georgia Tech, the University of South Carolina and North Carolina State. Again, I was very lucky to be surrounded by such great players and coaches. And, in spite of a grueling academic and practice schedule, I'm proud to say that I graduated *cum laude* with a bachelor's degree in Business Administration in four years. The self-discipline, peak performance and hard work learned from this experience would bode well for my career choice in the investment industry.

At 21, I barely survived a daunting interview process to become the youngest hire in my nationwide financial advisor training class at Merrill Lynch in Atlanta. The securities business is notorious for its high failure rate among new advisors and massive rejection was part of the game in those early prospecting years. To make matters worse, I was so young looking, I could have been mistaken for Opie on *The Andy Griffith Show!* But against the odds, and in spite of having no contacts and no real financial experience, I built a clientele from scratch through cold-calling, public speaking, networking, niche marketing and seminars and became a record-setting financial advisor. Courage and resilience became close companions.

A management and executive career in the financial services industry would follow in Southern California and later in Virginia, with many personal and professional ups and downs dotted along the way with each market cycle. I'll be sharing a few of those later. But as mid-life approached, after I got married and had kids, an interesting thing happened. Instead of settling down, I started getting restless. Sensing my discontent and ambivalence, my boss at the time asked me a simple yet haunting question one day, "What do you really want?"

All I knew then was that something was missing—the old carrots and sticks had lost their power over me. Somewhere along the way, my work had become empty, without real purpose or driving passion, disconnected from my core values, strengths and life goals. I had put too much emphasis on financial rewards and not enough on intrinsic rewards. I had made too many compromises and tradeoffs. I wasn't contributing in a way that I knew I could. I got stuck in a comfort zone. It was like I had been sleepwalking and something deep inside was trying to force me to wake up. It was that feeling that life is not a dress rehearsal, and I was on the wrong stage . . . wasting my time. I was meant to do something different with my life—I just had to figure out what that was.

What followed was part spiritual and part in-depth research. I started a relentless journey of personal and professional discovery that included: leaving my current job; reading numerous books; taking various aptitude and strength assessment tests; interviewing a wide range of people about different business and career opportunities; exploring new places to live; and taking long, introspective walks alone. I even took a month off to visit family I hadn't seen in years. This was not an overnight process but a highly productive and rewarding one. You see, part of my discovery process involved asking myself many of the same questions I will be inviting you to ask yourself in this book.

By experimenting with various steps to discover answers to these questions about how to live my own best life, I actually discovered how to coach others how to live their best life.

I began to see how, having spent many years doing financial and business coaching, I could combine elements of life coaching to make a deeper, more meaningful impact on the lives of others—to help people like you achieve ultimate success. This quest led to the launch of my own business, Bob David Live, Inc. (website: www.bobdavidlivecom), and to create this mission statement:

> To inspire, entertain, educate, coach and advise people in ways that maximize their potential, performance and happiness—to lead them on a journey of personal and professional development, purposeful contribution, financial success and lifelong goal achievement. And to have more fun and laughs along the way.

Before starting my own company, I had always worked with entrepreneurs as clients and had done many "entrepreneurial" things, but never totally walked in their shoes. Now, all that has changed. I enjoy the creative freedom and developing business processes and systems myself, but I have my moments where I laughingly lament, "So much to do, so few people to do it for me."

It was interesting to observe the reactions I got from different people after I launched my business. Some thought I was nuts starting a business during a recession. But from the start I was heartened to see how my own choices on my journey have positively influenced those around me—not just clients but friends, family and others in my life. Some are making radical career changes. Some are going out on their own. Some have set life goals for the first time. Others have made changes in their financial life. Many have begun programs to improve their health and fitness. Some have just started to challenge themselves to do, be and have more. They seem to be becoming more and more undaunted—just going for it.

My goal is to help you become more undaunted too. Let's get started.

1

Tossing Out Our Excuse Pillows

It's amazing to watch what happens to any of us when we come under pressure or are challenged to step up and deal with adversity. While we are all born with the tools we need to survive, some people make better use of what they have than others. We are rational creatures and when it comes to avoiding failure, our imaginations are limitless. It's the very things we do to avoid failure that actually end up setting us up for failure. So we spend time making "excuse pillows" to prepare ourselves psychologically to cushion our inevitable fall. We want to assure ourselves of making a nice soft landing. After all, if we are going to give up, we want to be fully prepared to offer enough excuses to enough people so we can feel better about ourselves when we quit trying. It's as if we can visualize those pillows protecting our egos.

Some folks have full-fledged excuse pillow factories, stuffed with the finest feathers. Do you prefer goose down or foam? Would you like those pillows with a custom-made pillow cover? Perhaps with your own message embroidered on the top? And the bigger the pillows the more justified we feel. It's all in preparation to cover our backsides. And we learn how to do it at an early age, usually surrounded by enablers that are supposed to be our family or friends. If we're not careful, reaching for these excuse pillows can become ingrained in our behavior. But when we commit to living *The Undaunted Life,* we learn that we can toss these excuse pillows right out the window.

First, we need to better understand where they come from and what they do. See if this illustration brings back any memories.

Imagine you're a freshman entering high school and you find yourself in an Algebra class. Let's say the teacher is a relatively unattractive older lady with a grumpy temperament—a real battle-axe. She's dressed sort of frumpy and talks with an irritating voice, lecturing on a topic she's not real passionate about and you're not really interested in. She has annoying mannerisms, distracting hand gestures and a boring monotone voice. She calls on you when you're not prepared, then embarrasses you in front of the entire class for not being prepared. Now, you have every reason to yell down to the excuse pillow factory floor and say, "All right boys, start up the assembly line, we've got a lot of material to work with today. Looks like we're going to have some big pillows to make and lots of them."

Pillow number 1: It's hard to learn with a teacher with that irritating voice.

Pillow number 2: The way she moves while she teaches is too distracting.

Pillow number 3: It's not just me; nobody is paying attention to her.

Pillow number 4: The subject matter is not something even relevant in the real world.

Pillow number 5: She doesn't like me now, so there's no way I'll get a good grade from her.

Pillow number 6: I've been labeled a problem, so even if I learn the material it will negatively impact my grade because she'll look for reasons to grade hard when it comes to any of my work.

Pillow number 7: If only I had the right classes prior to this one, I would be prepared to better learn this material.

Pillow number 8: This must be a bad school if they won't fire a teacher like this.

Pillow number 9: I've talked to other students and they all say she's a bad teacher.

Pillow number 10: I better prepare my parents for the bad news so they are not shocked when they see my report card.

And so the "excuse pillow" factory keeps working overtime to set the student up for failure in advance.

CULTURE OF "SOFTEES"

There is a drumbeat that seems to be getting louder and louder. Can you hear it? It's the sound of learned helplessness creeping into our culture bit by bit, one excuse pillow at a time. We see more and more individuals and industries shouting cries for "fairness," "bailouts" and "do-overs," with no thought to the long-term ramifications. My father is from what Tom Brokaw calls "the greatest generation" in part because they knew how to sacrifice instant gratification for something better later. When I hear talk about a "depression" I sometimes wonder if that's what our culture needs to get back to basics. We need to return to the fundamental truths of individual responsibility, success and achievement. We need to recognize that the government is not the answer. We need to stop giving up so easily when presented with an obstacle.

Perhaps one of the benefits of a difficult economic environment is to be forced to develop more resiliency, to learn not to fold when things don't go our way. In Malcolm Gladwell's book *Outliers*, he describes a situation in which a professor is exploring what makes some students more successful than others. In an experiment, students must attempt to solve a mathematical problem that he knows in advance will appear unsolvable. But even students of modest ability will be able to solve it as long as they don't give up trying. He writes, "Success is a function of persistence and doggedness and the willingness to work hard for 22 minutes to make sense of something most people would give up on after 30 seconds."

FRIDAYS AND MONDAYS

When I was a teenager, I made my first venture into the job market looking for summer work to buy a new stereo system for my "new used car." I soon discovered that university towns like Athens, Georgia, have a dearth of employment opportunities in the summer because most students go home and many of the businesses don't need extra help or even reduce their work force. Every door I knocked on seemed to be locked shut. The only people I knew getting jobs were those with some kind of inside connection orchestrated by their parents.

One day I heard that a new mall was being built in town. I drove past the construction site and found out that they were hiring for multiple worker types and to apply I would need to show up at 7:00 a.m. during the week. When I showed up, there must have been over 50 guys standing around waiting for the foreman to make some kind of announcement. After looking around at my competition, one thing stood out: I was not dressed for the part. They all had worn-looking blue jeans with work gloves stuck in the right back pocket, heavy-duty work boots and dirt under their fingernails. And there I stood in my preppy looking shirt, shorts and Top-Sider slip-on shoes. I overheard some snickers as they checked out this young kid who looked like he really didn't know what he was getting into. They were correct.

A scruffy guy named Bill appeared through the door of a construction side trailer parked just outside the site. He had on a hard hat and one of those "wife beater" T-shirts. You know, the kind with no sleeves. His skin looked like the leather on a football that had been knocked around in a mud bowl game between cross-town rivals and then left out in the hot sun to dry. I could barely understand what he was saying as he barked out commands in short bursts, "How many of ya 'er worked on a site 'fore?"

A slew of hands went up. Then he said "y all get oer her" and the ones that raised their hands were corralled behind the trailer. Then he said, "The rest of ya can go on 'ome."

While most of those not in the running lowered their heads and started toward the dirt parking lot, I was curious and decided to observe the next phase. The ones that made the first cut were asked to head one by one to the trailer where presumably they were asked more detailed questions. As the rejects came out, they would say something under their breath to rationalize why they didn't get hired: "They only want experienced bricklayers." "They only want experienced guys." "They don't want you if you're in any kind of union."

That night at the dinner table, my dad asked me how my job search was going. I proceeded to tell him all the reasons why I did not get the job. And guess what? I basically repeated all the things the rejected guys said. Then I started to launch into why I couldn't be expected to find a summer job in a university town unless he had some special strings he could pull like the fathers of my other friends who had already landed a job. I was making some pretty impressive excuse pillows.

Dad patiently listened, then asked me a simple question, "How bad do you want that stereo?" I told him all the reasons I wanted that stereo. Then he asked me "how much will it take to buy that stereo?" I told him. Then he said, "So when do you want that stereo?" I said by the time school started in the fall. Then he asked me "how much will you have to earn before taxes to come up with that amount?" We started calculating. "How much do you need to earn per hour with the time you have available?" He asked me how much they were paying the workers at the construction site. I told him that I found out there was a minimum wage at the site that was higher than the regular minimum wage. It finally dawned on me—I needed to land a construction job at that site to reach my goal. Even at their minimum rate, I could work just enough to make the money before summer football practice started. Dad then said, "I'll give you a little tip: the best time to get a job is Fridays or Mondays." He said those are the two days that people most often miss work or call in sick. I reminded him that it was Monday and there were over 50 guys waiting. Then he asked me if today was the first interview day. I said yes and he told me that I should keep showing up every morning and see what happens.

So I got up early again the next morning (Tuesday) and showed up at 7:00. Again, there were about 50 guys and it was basically a repeat of the previous day, with the same disgruntled comments from the rejected candidates. I tried again Wednesday morning, but then I began making more excuse pillows. "This job really wasn't going to prepare me in any way for anything so maybe it was a waste of time anyway." "It might even be a dangerous place to work—what with all the nails and equipment. And let's don't forget the sun. I'm fair skinned—I might be planting the seeds for skin cancer down the road. . . . "By the time I pay all the taxes . . ."

Oh, by the way, all football players were "strongly encouraged' to work out with weights and run at our high school during the summer months. So no matter how strenuous the job, I had to find time to work out every weekday. This is when I started to hear my football coach's voice in my head saying, "Winners never quit and quitters never win." So I made up my mind I was going to go back the next morning, and keep going back. I even cut the arms out of a T-shirt, put on the most worn- looking jeans I could find and ditched the slip-ons in favor of some old tennis shoes. I made enough of an impression to get a response from Bill. "You've been coming here every morning, haven't you?" he asked. When I said yes, he asked, "Have ya ever worked on a site?" I said no. He said, "Well, we can't use you. Sorry." Then he suddenly walked away, shouting some obscenities at a guy operating the cement mixer.

Now, when I went home that night, I could at least feel good about my effort. After all, I had gone way beyond what most teenagers would have done in terms of handling rejection. Over the weekend, a friend and I went to the car stereo store. I saw the exact unit I wanted but it seemed all was lost at this point. Whatever few jobs that were available for the summer were no doubt taken. Maybe that stereo wasn't worth buying anyway. When I went to bed that night, I looked over at my alarm clock. I was exhausted from working out every day, so why not give myself a break and sleep in late in the morning? But something in my gut told me to give it yet another try Monday morning.

When I arrived at the site, I walked straight to the trailer where I knew Bill would be having his morning coffee. When he saw me he said, "Boy, am I glad you showed up. We had a laborer not make it in this morning. Can you handle a shovel?" I was hired on the spot! Now

I can tell you that a "laborer" was basically a go-fer guy—someone who does what they tell you. In my case, I would end up spending most of my time being an assistant to a bricklayer. But I learned many valuable lessons that summer—two that stand out: 1) the power of persistence; and 2) I never wanted to have to do this kind of physical labor again! This would serve as a real motivator for me in my schoolwork when fall came around, and for any new goal or experience I would target.

THE "ADVENTURE MINDSET"

When you are preparing to experience something new, there is a fine line between being anxious about it and feeling excited about it. This is especially true during challenging economic times. If you're anxious you may find yourself grabbing for those excuse pillows. So it helps to develop what I call an adventure mindset—one of positive expectancy and willingness to try something new. Are you mastering the changes necessary to survive in this environment? In order for you to adapt to any new environment, you have to be willing to change your behavior and try some new things. It's vital that we all become action oriented and create opportunities, rather than wait for on opportunity to come to your doorstep. You want to avoid "paralysis by analysis."

In nature it's relatively easy to spot the survivors because by definition the ones that didn't make it simply are not around anymore. So we can learn from those who have already figured out many of the basics. Don't try to reinvent the wheel if you don't have to. The best way to prepare for a new direction, a new journey, is to learn from those who have successfully navigated that path—those with experience in living with an adventure mindset. When you are looking for ways to survive and thrive in a poor economic environment, for example, take the time to identify and get to know all the "insiders" if at all possible. If you are thinking of changing industries, talk with someone who made a similar change and became successful. If you are going through a difficult time in your personal life, such as divorce or bankruptcy, seek out individuals who have gone through the pain. They can share with you pitfalls to avoid and tips to come out the other side stronger and wiser.

PURSUIT OF EXCELLENCE VS. EGALITARIANISM

One of the things I really love about being an American is our history of self-reliance and the success stories of people who come to this country with little more than a dream and the clothes on their back to make it against overwhelming odds. Though I'm not naïve about the advantages and privileges enjoyed by certain elite members of our society, history confirms that most of the millionaires in this country did it in one generation. That says that there must be something right about our system. I'm drawn to a system that does not guarantee success for everyone. There is something empowering about a meritocracy, where there is no limit or ceiling to how high you can climb. It's a system that honors and glorifies the pursuit of excellence.

But there is a definite movement afoot to challenge that system and even replace it with one of entitlement and mediocrity. Excuse pillows for all! I disdain that notion and a system that stymies the spirit of competition. It's the spirit of competition that makes us stronger, not some silly notion of egalitarianism, which is basically a system promoting "equality of results" for all. I'd much rather live in a society that allows failure than one that promotes mediocrity. I'm reminded of one of my favorite quotes from the legendary football coach Vince Lombardi:

> "The quality of a person's life is in direct proportion to their commitment to excellence."

It's become popular now in our schools to pass out trophies to all the kids regardless of performance. This is done ostensibly to raise the self-esteem of the children and foster more teamwork. I'm all in favor of the latter, but it's the former I take issue with. In the short run it might feel good to have every child go home with a trophy. But the lesson they learn from that is that no matter what the quality of my effort, no matter my individual effort or team results, I will get recognized. This is not a healthy message at all. It can breed learned helplessness.

CHOICES AND CONSEQUENCES

If you are a parent you know just how important it is to teach your kids to understand and appreciate the universal law of choices and consequences. Every decision we make has a consequence. It's amazing how many people never seem to get this. As the parent of two young children, I have come to believe that one of the best things we can do as parents is to allow our children to fail, then teach them what to do when that happens. This is far different for the "helicopter" parents that swing into action when there is a crisis to bail out their kids and blame their kids' behavior or failure on something outside their control.

My wife and I have seen this many times. One of our son's former classmates had parents that did not believe in disciplining their child, and eventually this came back to bite them and the child. We had socialized with them on more than one occasion and everyone knew that this boy was struggling with discipline at school. Once I witnessed this boy hit another child right under his parents' nose, and the father's response was so weak it was shocking. His parents would even brag how they really didn't believe in being too strict and wanted their son to be "free to express himself." Who's in charge here anyway? If you want to permanently cripple a child's life potential, let them think they are running things at an early age. Subconsciously, that is a very scary place to be. It's like letting kids eat candy all day. They might like it. They may think you're a lot of "fun." They may think you are "cool." But you're not being a real parent. You are enabling bad behavior and retarding their growth. You are encouraging them to be dependent rather than independent—to make excuse pillows. To be a successful parent, you must help them learn that failure is as indispensable to ultimate success as carbon is to steel.

SECRETS OF "FAILURE"

The paradox is that the people who fail the most end up being the most successful, as long as they grow from that experience and improve as a result. We are so afraid of seeing our children fail that we step in right at the moment when there is an opportunity for them to grow from the experience. Let's take the example of the overly eager parent. I remember once coming home from school in seventh grade and telling my parents that I needed to create a science project to compete in a school-wide science fair. There was pretty broad latitude in deciding what project to tackle, and I was looking for all the help I could get. I certainly didn't care about learning any life lessons. Because my parents were not science oriented, they were not sure what to do, but the fact that it was a "contest" got them thinking. My dad finally suggested that a colleague of his at the university might be able to help because he had a "science orientation."

They arranged for him to come over for dinner one night and afterwards I sat down with him and told him the goal. We did come up with what I thought was a pretty cool experiment showing how water pressure worked, but this wasn't just my project now. It was "our" project and this adult's ego was on the line based on the results. Over several evenings together, frankly with him doing most of the heavy lifting, the project was complete. I felt pretty good about it. He was invited to the science fair event along with my parents. When we arrived, I will never forget the look on their faces when they saw some of these displays. There were three distinct categories of work:

1. Project where it was clear the student had done it on their own.
2. Project where it was clear the student had some help.
3. Project where it was clear an adult had basically done the whole thing.

To be fair, mine fell into category two. And the ones in category three were really impressive—some with moving parts, animated models and detailed graphic designs. As students we were all going around challenging the kids that we knew didn't do it themselves. How could the parents (or the kids themselves for that matter) say with a straight face they actually did those projects by themselves? Here was the amazing part: there must have been an assumption of the honor system with the fair because the exhibit that won really was the best. But here is the key question as it relates to success vs. failure: Who were the real winners here? I would argue that the real winners were the ones that did the projects all by themselves yet lost and felt the sting of defeat. They walked away with something more important than the trophy:

1. The pride of knowing they did it themselves.
2. An important life lesson: sometimes you will not win because the competition is not fighting fair.

You can cry foul all day long but nobody is really listening. The fact is that when a student goes into the real world they will encounter countless situations that are "unfair." And, if they have developed the habit of blame and making excuses, it will haunt them the rest of their lives. It's like in life there is a wall and you have to get over that wall no matter what. There will be folks taller than you who can see the wall more clearly. There may be those who can jump higher to get off to a faster start over the wall. There may be those who can afford to buy a ladder to help them climb it. There are those who are smarter who find a better way to get over it or go around it. But, just when you think you have an excuse as to why you are not getting over the wall, you look over and see a tiny boy or girl with one arm making it over. All those excuse pillows get torn to shreds.

EFFORT AND REWARD

Think about the well-meaning parent who did all the work to get the trophy for their kid. Imagine now in high school when they are asked to do another project but, for whatever reason, Mommy and Daddy are not around to do it for them. Now they don't have the psychological confidence that comes from being tested. Their first response will be to expect someone else to do it for them. This habit may perpetuate itself throughout life into their career, family life, etc. Are they more or less likely to look to the government for help? Are they more or less likely to blame the system when something goes wrong?

They never really get the connection between effort and reward—and the reality that the reward may not always be the trophy. It's like the Olympic athlete who works hard for years to compete in a sport, then ends up winning a bronze metal. But they win on so many other levels getting to that place. One of the best ways to teach children about effort and reward is to start with "baby steps." Focus on recognizing progress along the way. We are creatures of habit and we learn those habits early in life.

I remember when my son first started to crawl, we would put his favorite toy a few feet from him and them cheer him on as he made progress. When he finally reached and grabbed the toy, we clapped and cheered. People who succeed in life understand the price they have to pay in advance of getting rewarded. I've met so many people in my life who think they can be successful without paying the price of success. They believe that if only they are assured the reward, then they will put forth the effort. They want the outcome already laid out in advance. And wherever you see an individual, a family, a business or a culture that has lost the work ethic and the link between effort and reward, you can be assured of its ultimate failure.

WHEN IT COMES TO SUCCESS, LOOKS CAN BE DECEIVING . . .

If you show me someone who doesn't have much failure experience, I'll show you someone without much success experience. But here's the difference: they often don't seem disheartened or victimized by the situation or the circumstances. And because they are not making excuses, and because they choose to interpret their situation as a temporary setback, it's assumed they have not actually failed. We think they have the golden touch. We believe that they will be just fine.

What they really have is a system of beliefs about themselves and a success strategy that they have learned from the crucible of experience. They carry around a self-image about what they can or can't do. They have a certain level of references in their past that support their beliefs. You could put two individuals with similar ability but with very different beliefs into the same environment and often get radically different results. For example, let's take two siblings who grow up in the same upscale neighborhood yet have radically different experiences directly related to growing up there. Assume their family owns one of the lower-end homes in the development. One kid believes that because they don't have as nice a house or as many toys, or don't ride around in as nice a car, they would be far better off living in a less affluent neighborhood. The other kid, on the other hand, sees this as an opportunity. They see the fact that their family just barely squeaked in there, a real blessing in disguise. Now they can be exposed to a nicer class of people and be around more educated folks, gaining from interaction with more accomplished neighbors. It's all in the way the circumstances are interpreted.

LEARNING HOW TO WIN

It's too bad we are not all born with a manual that tells us what we really need to know to win in the game of life. While it's true that success is the result of prior failures, it's also true that people and organizations who win in life and the marketplace do have a "secret sauce," a way of doing things that separates them from the pack. Expectations play a big role. When I was in the marching band with my saxophone, there were certain things I was expected to do. I went to two-a-day band practice and had to learn how to play on the move. But when I was in the stands watching our football team go undefeated and win the state championship, it was clear that something special was happening on that field and it didn't just happen automatically. Somebody was teaching those players how to win. Somebody was leading the group. Someone was figuring out how to get the most of each player down on that field. Someone was putting together a weekly game plan to beat the opponent. Someone was organizing a lot of moving parts.

And, perhaps most importantly, somebody was raising the bar—teaching the pursuit of excellence. The reality is that in life and in business there is a scoreboard. And there are winners and losers. When somebody gets the business, the other businesses don't. When somebody lands a contract, somebody else did not. This is the way of the world. And it's a good thing. Imagine a world where there were no winners and losers. It would be a race to the bottom. Imagine a world where there were no rewards for improvement, for getting better for scoring more points, racking up more sales, executing better than the competition. At best it's a "race for the middle." If you want to be more successful, take the time to study success.

12:00 NOON SUMMER WORKOUTS

One of the habits I formed when I was training for football in high school was getting stronger when the situation demanded it. For example, my coach had summer sessions called 12:00 Noon Workouts. The idea was that psychologically, if you were willing to come onto the field in the middle of the day in the hot summer sun to go through a brutal workout, you were forging the kind of mental and physical toughness that would pay off when the game was on the line in the fourth quarter. No excuse pillows here! As Vince Lombardi said, "Fatigue makes cowards of us all." Coach Henderson was a master motivator. Think about the mental training going on here: "If I go to these workouts, that means I'm somebody that sacrifices my comfort and shade to expose myself to grueling conditions. But I'm willing to do that because I can then brag about what I just did." Our self-esteem grew because our coach found a way to set the bar higher. He understood one of the most powerful drives in all of us: to be part of something bigger than ourselves and accomplish something grand. And he set up the price to be paid in advance so that when the time came, we would have that reference to boost our confidence. If we could survive this, we could take whatever the other team had to dish out.

The same can be done in your personal and business life. What would happen if you raised the bar? What are your competitors doing that you can do even better? What can you do to make a dramatic statement to the world and to yourself that might propel you to higher heights? How can you rally your team around a cause? What are you doing to pursue excellence? What are you doing to put more points on the board in your business, your career, in your personal relationships? The more you make this kind of thinking the focus of your approach, the less you will ever find yourself reaching for an excuse pillow.

2

Emonomics™: How to Master Your Emotions in any Economy

Most of us are aware of how the overall economy impacts our spending and savings. When the economy is doing well, we tend to spend more and, when the economy is doing poorly, we tend to spend less. What many of us don't realize, though, is just how much we allow the economy to influence our emotions and consequently our decision-making across the board. Over 70 percent of our economy is tied to consumer spending so these swings in how we feel about the economy are a big deal. But I have come to believe that beyond that obvious link lies a highly dysfunctional relationship between the economy and how we feel, causing destructive decision-making and missed opportunities.

WHAT WAS I THINKING? THE PARADOX OF FINANCIAL SUCCESS AND FAILURE

It was the fall of 2000, and my life could not have been better. I had just bought a new house in the exclusive California city of Indian Wells, right behind my office (I could have walked to work). My portfolio was skyrocketing. I was one of those lucky guys that you never read about but knew were out there during the dot-com boom. I had put a large chunk of change on a single stock that went up 30 fold (that's 3,000 percent) in less than one year. The interesting thing is that the stock made that move with very little fanfare, compared to shooting stars like Yahoo and JDS Uniphase. I had met my future wife, and I was recognized as one of the top branch managers in the country. I was making great money. And I was shopping for a new car. The desert is a beautiful place, almost surreal at times, and I had a beautiful swimming pool with a fantastic view of the San Jacinto Mountains. We would sit in the hot tub when the temperature started to drop and drink margaritas while we talked about our future life together.

Then, over the next 24 months, my world would turn upside down as the dot-com bubble burst and the economy went into recession. My portfolio tanked and, to make matters worse, I inconveniently had a mid-life career crisis. I would be tested in ways that I'd never been tested. It seems that no matter how much we've been tested the next test is always just different enough to force us into developing new strategies, new attitudes and new levels of resiliency. I remember going through all kinds of emotions during that time, through both the boom and the subsequent bust.

But I certainly learned a lot. I began to recognize how being in the financial services industry my entire career had given me a front-row seat to the way economic cycles are linked to how we feel. As I looked back over my career, I discovered how there seemed to be a pattern in my thoughts and behavior directly linked to the economy. Many observers could point out, "Duh, we all know that already." But there was more to the equation. If the economy is the body then surely the financial markets are the blood pumping through the veins. How capital flows can tell you what you need to know about the patient. Everything else can be working fine but if your blood has a problem, it's sure to impact the whole body. So it really doesn't matter if the tail is wagging the dog or not. There is just an inseparable link that can be observed when you track the financial markets and the economy.

When a doctor wants to know how you are doing, what's the first thing they want to do? Have your blood checked. The paradox is that financial success itself often sows the seeds for later financial failure. Maybe it's as simple as too much greed. But I think there is much more going on here than meets the eye. When I think back to mistakes I've made in my own decision-making process, one of the first questions that comes to my mind is: What was I thinking? And what was the feeling that I failed to understand as a driving force for my actions?

The whole universe operates in cycles. Our solar system, our seasons, even our bodies have natural cycles that can be understood and measured. Farmers know when to plant and when to harvest. Birds know when to fly south for the winter. Our ancestors knew to fix their shelter when the sun is shining, not after it starts to rain. But for some reason, we don't seem to have good intuitive decision-making when it comes to money and finances. For example, it's no coincidence that there is a huge disparity between the average return of a mutual fund and the average return of a mutual fund holder. The difference is that most fund buys happen at the top and most fund sells happen at the bottom. There is a perverse relationship between the price of an investment and the level of enthusiasm among investors to pay that price. When things are going up, we more readily buy. We love "track records," which by definition are rearview mirrors. Like diamonds and perfume, the higher the price of an investment goes, the more attractive it appears. The lower a price of an investment drops, the less confidence we have in purchasing it. When things are great in our jobs, we spend more and save less. When things are tight, we spend less and save more. Shouldn't the best time to save be when you are making the most money, not the least? And isn't it true that the best time to buy something is when it's on sale? We wait all year for that annual sale at Nordstrom's but won't touch a stock when it's marked down.

I believe that by having a better objective understanding of the link between the economic cycle and how you feel, you can make better, more objective decisions. Forewarned is forearmed. Then, once you gain that awareness of those cycles—no matter the length or severity—you can successfully develop counter strategies to prevent making mistakes in the heat of those moments. You can be empowered to take advantage of opportunities during those times. Like buying snow shovels in summer, you can make smarter moves over the length of the cycle.

So, are you ready to learn another valuable tool in living *The Undaunted Life?*

7 EMOTIONAL STATES LINKED WITH THE BUSINESS CYCLE

1. Confidence

This is the stage where the fundamentals of the economy appear to be sound enough for there to be optimism in the future. The news flow has its usual focus on some negatives, but there are enough positives in data and boardrooms that you see hiring. You see new initiatives, new ventures being launched. There is usually a hot new thing that gets everyone's attention. There is faith in the future, a willingness to take some risk. A feeling that it's OK to stick your toe in the water, the temperature is fine. Financial advisors are upbeat during this phase, mirroring the mood of their clients. There is actually a nice balance during this phase between the demands and expectations of investors and the reasonable recommendations of financial advisors.

Here's a scenario illustrating how this might play out. A client named Joe just had a CD mature and is interested in earning a higher return. The talk at the country club isn't necessarily all about the virtues of stocks but there is an absence of trash talking and horror stories about equities. Joe has been reading in the paper how the economy seems to be showing a good head of steam and, coincidentally, he's in line for a promotion at his company. They just announced a new deferred compensation plan for higher paid executives and he's signing up. Joe's never been comfortable with individual stocks because of the money he lost with a penny stockbroker years ago. But he's read enough about mutual funds to think that some kind of professionally-managed account might make sense for his CD money.

The advisor, Jennifer, greets Joe and gets an update on his situation. She already has his IRA rollover from his previous job but this amount of money will clearly take the relationship to another level, tripling the amount of his assets under her management. She does some financial planning work and projects what he needs to accumulate to reach his goals. She introduces him to a fee-based account using multiple money managers with Jennifer as the financial quarterback, directing the overall asset allocation and reviewing the performance of each individual manager. She shows the track record of each of these managers and projects what that return would mean for him if he did just "average." Everything is "sunshine on the meadow" at this stage—everyone is expecting good things. Behind the scenes, Jennifer's business is picking up. She is starting to get some referrals from existing clients who trust her judgment and who have seen an improvement in their results. If you were measuring client behavior influence on a scale of 1 to 10 with 1 being the lowest and 10 the highest, Jennifer is at a solid 7 right now.

2. Greed

Now let's fast-forward 18 months out. The bull market is not only in full swing, its enthusiasm has become contagious. The mood of investors is almost giddy. The news flow is so good that investors who missed the boat are feeling really, really stupid. I would argue that it is more psychologically painful to watch a missed opportunity succeed than to watch what you thought was a winner drop. They say that fear of loss is stronger than desire for gain. But that is incomplete. What makes greed so insidious, if not bridled, is the fact that you desperately don't want the ride to end. And if you are one of the few still sitting at the train station, you are feeling not only like you are missing all the fun but something far deeper than that: you feel insulated and alone. There is a social dimension to investing that is under-appreciated.

I've seen this dynamic play out so many times and in so many ways. For example, I have an uncanny ability to make major purchases at what prove to be market tops. But this is understandable. Because I'm in the industry, I make more income when the markets are going up. Therefore I have more discretionary spending dollars. And the other thing that happens is that we begin extrapolating recent performance way out into the future. We tend to think that the most logical conclusion is that there is somehow a predictive quality to recent trends. We believe that "the trend is your friend." And surprise, surprise—we have the most friends when things are up. We feel good about ourselves and our future. But now we begin fantasy thinking. I can remember going to "client appreciation events" and watching expensive bottles of wine being uncorked. I remember one of my advisors informing me that his client was leaving him after 10 years because he only made him 30 percent last year and his buddy made 60 percent.

3. Denial

Understand that I'm not passing judgments on the merits or moral standing of each of these stages, simply identifying the best word to describe how we feel at different points in the cycle. Only by bringing some level of objectivity can we create a model that can then be used as a tool to develop strategies to improve our bottom line results, leading to more success in all areas of our lives.

In this phase, the bubble has burst but very few actually heard it the moment it happened. Only through the rearview mirror can we accurately assess the exact timing of when things took a turn. There is almost always some watershed event or catalyst that becomes identified with the change from one stage to the next. I remember once returning from a conference speaking engagement at midnight on a Friday night eager to see my family, only to discover my car had a flat tire. Fortunately I am a AAA cardholder and with a simple phone call was able to get on the road again within an hour or so. But when I took the old tire into the shop the next day, the mechanic walked out of the garage carrying a three-inch nail and said, "This is why you got a flat. You probably hit this several days ago and didn't even know it when it happened. Then the leak finally took out enough air for you to notice." When I think back, there were some clues, like a slight pull to one side. There may have even been a warning light but I was too busy to notice. It's the same thing at this stage. Because the good times have been going for a while, our first reaction is denial. We see what we chose to see. There is a built-in bias that goes something like this: Whatever action we have taken becomes the right one merely as a result of us making that choice.

In Dr. Robert Cialdini's book, *Influence,* he calls this concept "commitment and consistency." It essentially says that once we decide on a particular course of action we feel compelled to believe and act in ways that are consistent with that course of action. So, for example, when we buy a stock that starts going down, we may rationalize that it's just because of a "correction" in the market or a temporary dip in economic activity—couldn't be any issue with the company. I'm a smart person, therefore I make good decisions, therefore I'm right and the market is wrong. . . . Denial takes many forms. It might be as subtle as not paying attention because you've been right for long enough in the past so you have residual confidence and greed from the prior two stages. It might be that you have not yet seen any outward signs of a change. We all hear stories of heart attack victims that seemed just fine that morning, then "bam"—a heart attack hits that afternoon. And when they go in they discover plaque that's been building in the arteries for a while. There is also a pride factor that plays to the social aspect of investing that tells us not to get shaken out of the market at the first sign of trouble. Aren't you gutsy enough to handle a little volatility? After all, volatility makes you outsized returns over time, right? And long term, it's the "sitting" not the trading that makes money, right? There is no free lunch and so this is when investors get to experience why they can make higher returns. At this stage we see some negative news popping up but overall there is more hope than objective analysis.

4. Fear

This is the most powerful four-letter word in the human experience. We know that the fastest way to change a person's behavior in the short term is through fear.

Exhibit 1 Chart

Psychologists will tell you that the fear of loss is stronger than the desire for gain—but only to a point. Those of us here now owe our existence partly to some brave ancestors who decided it was better to risk their lives killing wild beasts for food than to starve. But in modern times, and for the purposes of this model, FEAR is the dominant emotion. And it's hardwired in our "fight or flight" response—even as much as we would like to deny its influence in so-called modern times. In certain circumstances it is automatic. And I might add it's served us well as a survival tool. Without it, our ancestors might not have instinctively avoided the dangers in their environment, ensuring the survival of their genetic code. When it comes to investing, this is the stage where the most mistakes are made by far.

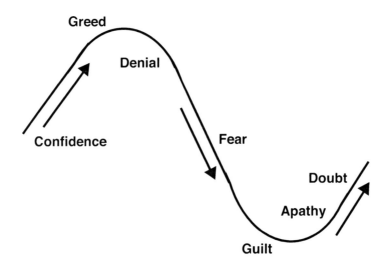

By definition, this is where those in denial finally pull their heads out of the sand and start to look around at all the "evidence" of why things have started to really drop.

This is marked by alarming one-day price swings in the markets. Because of its relative importance as a stage, I want to introduce three "sub-stages" within FEAR.

Shock. As investors move from denial to fear, the initial wave of emotion can best be described as "shock." It's like a death in the family. What is our reaction when we first hear the news? We may have been in denial about all the things leading up to this moment, but nothing prepares us quite like facing the music. Nothing stings quite like emerging from our cave to see what's really been happening in our environment. In the case of investors, it's the reality sinking in for the first time as you finally open your monthly statements and see just how far things have gone down. If you've been ignoring the news, you start to tune in. If your advisor has been cautious, you start to understand why. If your advisor has been telling you "think long term" you are starting to question that wisdom. You start to notice all the evidence that this is going to impact your financial goals, that this might not be temporary. The news is taking a decided turn for the worse. Talk of recession is not just speculation, it appears imminent. You begin hearing that people are being laid off. You actually know someone who just lost their job. At the end of this phase you begin to feel the pull to take some kind of action. Most people, after witnessing a bomb, instinctively start to anticipate the possibility of the next one—so they start the next phase.

Panic. As an advisor and a branch manager, I knew many clients over the years who were excellent anecdotal barometers for what was going on in the minds of other investors. And they were usually excellent contrary indicators. When they finally called excited to buy, you wanted to consider selling. When they finally couldn't stand the pain any more and came in to "sell everything" and panic sell, that usually marked at least a short-term bottom in the market. This phase is often irrational. I can't tell you how many times I've had conversations where people actually thought the S&P 500 was going to 0, and 100 percent of their savings with it. As recent experience has taught us, stocks can and do go to zero. But that is why diversification is so critical. We'll get to that in a moment. For now, I want to further explore how "panic" impacts the psyche.

One of its manifestations is a preoccupation with worst-case scenarios. As panic sets in we actually begin to play out what-if scenarios that are not grounded in reality. Just as the greed stage leads to irrational fantasy thinking and extrapolating recent returns into infinity, panic leads to irrational fear that limits our options. Not only is the news bad but we're now conditioned to expect more bad news. The message is: run for cover. Using the battlefield metaphor, we hear calls of "incoming" as we develop a bunker mentality. I've seen advisors panic along with their clients. They can't take it anymore. There is also a physiological need to do something, anything. And so we see investors selling this or buying that to feel better. They say, "Well, at least I didn't just sit there and take it—I did something about it." Never mind that sitting might be the best course of action, as long as it's made consciously and rationally. The big problem with making any decision in the panic stage is we usually don't have all of our faculties. It goes back to our cave dweller days when there was no time to contemplate, reflect or analyze. Whatever is causing the pain, just kill it. If it's an investment, then sell it. That's the way to get rid of it. It's like you've been hit with an arrow: the best way to heal is to first remove the arrow.

Blame. After panic, there is tremendous internal pressure to rationalize that action or that decision. We will go out of our way to prove that what we did was justified under the circumstances—even smart, wise, prudent, etc. But invariably, there needs to be a scapegoat for our tale. We need to have a bad guy in our story to make us look like more of the hero. We seek out somebody or something to blame other than ourselves. It might be an advisor. It might be a family member. It might be a friend or coworker, a teacher, a doctor, etc. It might be Jim Cramer on TV or some other media or authority figure. This may progress to larger group blame, such as the company, the school, the church or even the government or the president. This is about pointing fingers and feeling better because if it's somebody else's fault then by definition it's not my fault, right? I've talked with clients who have their own personal horror stories about bad times or investment losses that more often than not has some victim feel to it. It's as if they are scarred by a past experience and emphatically blame their circumstance on something outside their own control. In my career as a branch manager, I've seen lawsuits directed at advisors and their firms. And there are legitimate situations where the recommended investments were unsuitable. But it's also true that a number of these suits are about rationalizing losses. The husband lost the money and needs to blame someone else so his wife doesn't blame him. Or the widow who knew what she was doing but conveniently gets amnesia about her knowledge of what was happening in her portfolio to avoid facing responsibility.

5. Guilt

As time goes by, after fear has been the predominant emotional driver in our decision-making process, we begin to reflect back on what has happened with some perspective. We start feeling guilty about what transpired, even ashamed in some situations. It's much like being in the heat of an argument and realizing later that maybe the other side had some good points. As the economy and the markets start to bottom out, we examine what we did or didn't do and the second-guessing begins. Maybe we panicked. Maybe we made a hasty decision (a job change or divorce, etc.). We may feel overwhelmed with grief. "My portfolio died at my own hand." I remember once convincing a client to "dollar cost average" during the 1990 bear market. He was steadily putting the same amount of money into a mutual fund like clockwork every month. The market kept going down, but that was the idea—that he was getting more and more shares for the same amount of money. When the market turns up you then have lowered your overall cost and thus maximize your profit long term. It's the best way to make volatility your friend.

The problem was, he was watching the wrong thing. He kept looking in the paper at the news and his share price. Finally he called me and said, "I know what you're going to say—that I should keep buying. But I can't take it. Please stop the automatic contributions." So I complied. But amazingly (or not so amazingly—remember those contrary indicators I alluded too earlier?) the market turned up right when the Gulf War started a few weeks later and, because he had made the decision to stop, the last thing he wanted to tell me was to start it up again. He was psychologically stuck. Over the next year, he transferred his account. And it had nothing to do with the quality of advice he got. Had he stuck to the strategy, he would have been in great shape. He never even gave me a head's-up phone call that he was leaving. I never spoke with him again, but I can guarantee you besides his loss of pride, the dominant emotion at play had to be his own guilt and shame for not sticking to the original plan. He simply couldn't face me going forward. No matter what happened next, the relationship had been contaminated and in his mind the only way to cleanse it was to move to another advisor. Only then could he be freed of that haunting guilt that often comes from making poor decisions.

6. Apathy

After dealing with guilt, we see that this whole experience has left not only scars but also exhaustion. One sure sign that we are ready for the next bull market is that people begin to totally lose interest in what's happening in the economy and in the stock market. I recall thinking that the housing market had to be topping when the TV show *Flip This House* began to air. Going forward, some of the signs of investors becoming truly apathetic might be when previously popular shows such as *Mad Money* with Jim Cramer or *Fast Money* were canceled. People will have found other things to obsess about, other ways to spend their time. The whole culture will have moved on. We will all have lost our patience. I had a recent conversation with an advisor who is a friend of mine. Usually, part of our conversation involves what's happening in the economy and the stock market. A funny thing happened: he wanted to tell me about how he just entered a chili-cooking contest. He told me how he had spent six hours on it over the weekend and he detailed the unique ingredients that could make his chili a winner. He had changed the subject.

News fatigue sets in at this stage and we find ourselves becoming interested in other activities. Many sociologists tell us this is a good thing because it forces values clarification. After all, over half the U.S. population owns stock in some form. We have become a nation of investors. We have an investor culture and it's a large block of votes. Since the early '80s we've seen more and more people and businesses look to the stock market to gauge whether it's a good time to invest in anything, whether it's a stock or a second business location. When there is apathy, there is a dearth of confidence in the future. You could also argue that by the time this stage runs its course everyone who was going to sell has already sold. We're now beyond negative media telling us how bad it is—it's obvious that there is no value in continuing to beat a dead horse. One condition that has to be met for a bottom in stocks to be reached is that they have to stop going down. They don't have to turn up, they just have to stop going down. If you have held on this long and weathered the fear (shock, panic, blame) parts of the cycle, you might as well hold on. Buyers at this point are arguably the most patient because they are buying not because they see a catalyst for things to move higher, they just see the value in certain stocks too tempting to pass up. These "value buyers" are the only ones left doing the buying, but the tug-of-war with the sellers has resulted in a sort of stalemate. The few sellers left have run out of stock to sell and the few buyers have agreed to pay that clearance price. It may be dividend yields; it might be book value; it might be price to earnings or price to cash flow. Stock at this point ends up in much stronger hands. That's why it's the last phase before things start to turn up . . .

7. Doubt

If you live in a part of the world that has harsh cold winters or scorching hot summers, then you know how important it is to appreciate where you are in the weather cycle. If you live in Minnesota and you wake up one morning to a foot of fresh snow, how you feel about that might depend on whether it's the beginning of winter or the end. If you typically dread the onset of winter, that initial snowfall is a sign of things to come—the first of many—and you know the temperature is only going to get colder. When I lived in the desert of Southern California, we used to get a ton of "snowbirds" who would leave their cold-weather homes to live in the desert for the winter, then go back home for the other months. We would hear clients bragging about how cold it was back home or how much snow The Weather Channel said hit their hometown, all while playing golf on a sun-drenched, 80-degree day on a lush golf course with neighbors cheering them on between sips of their umbrella drinks from their fully furnished outdoor patios lining the course. But imagine if you had no way of knowing whether it was December or March? Those four months would make a lot of difference in how you might anticipate the change of seasons, wouldn't it? Because if you live in Minnesota in the winter and you get a warm day in December, it's far different than getting a warm day in March. When you get the warm day in March, it's a sign that winter is coming to an end and you begin to eagerly anticipate that turn. You get excited—spring fever. But without knowledge of the calendar, you would have major doubt. You wouldn't trust that spring was around the corner.

We desert natives actually had the opposite problem than the snowbirds. We would all dread the onset of summer where temperatures frequently reached 115 to 120 degrees. And the sweltering humidity in August made it unbearable to be outside at all during the day. My view on the desert summers was "you always know when it's time for summer again—it's just when you finally get used to the beautiful winter and spring weather and your memory of last summer's oppressive heat finally fades." Using the desert weather pattern metaphor, doubt is when it's September and the summer heat is still there in full force but the turn is happening under the radar—it's just been going on long enough that by the end of the month you start to see small signs that only a seasoned veteran sees. It's only 107 instead of 115—still damn hot, but the edge is starting to come off at the margin.

Stocks are supposed to be "discounting mechanisms," meaning that the present value of a share is supposed to represent the present value of all future cash flows associated with owning that business. Novice investors are shocked when they see stocks going up yet the news is still bad. This is normal. We used to see this in the desert real estate sale cycle. Invariably the best time to buy a home in the desert was in the middle of summer when nobody wanted to live there. The best time to sell was in January when everyone wanted to live there. But there comes a point where that balance between buyers and sellers reaches equilibrium. It's important to remember:

7 SURVIVAL TACTICS FOR EACH STAGE OF THE CYCLE

Now that you've been introduced to the Emonomics Model, and understand the basic concepts of how the economy impacts how you feel depending on where we are in the business cycle, the next obvious question is: OK, now what? Well, the purpose of introducing you to this model is first to empower you with some awareness about what is going on around you and how that affects how you feel, which in turn impacts the quality of your decisions. What can you do to counteract the gravitational force of these emotions linked to the cycles to improve your decisions? How can you take back control of how you feel, rather than having your emotions controlled by these cycles beyond your control?

The answer is by consciously developing specific survival tactics in advance so that you know where you need to focus your energy. Once you're able to properly identify where you are in the cycle, you can act to neutralize and even capitalize on what's happening. Rather than become a victim of these cycles you become a master of them. When everyone else is confused and scattered, you are clear and purposeful. Instead of saying to yourself, "What was I thinking?" now you know what you are going to be thinking and "forewarned is forearmed." You can get prepared for whatever comes your way. The most successful people, families and organizations anticipate the future, not just react to it. In chess they call it counter moves. In football it's called having a well-thought-out game plan before walking onto the field. Based on my years of working with clients and coaching advisors, I want to offer you seven survival tactics that correspond to each of the seven dominant emotions we experience in the cycle.

1. Confidence—Preparedness

Like buying snow shovels in the summer, being prepared is being smart. This simple, straightforward Boy Scout motto is so foundational yet so ignored by most people. To put this in proper context, let's first revisit *confidence*. Of all the 7 emotional states related to the business cycle, confidence is arguably the most powerful and predictive state of mind that most impacts behavior. When we have confidence we move forward, and when we don't we won't—it's a simple as that. There is a reason that we see official economic models based on confidence such as "Michigan consumer sentiment" or "consumer confidence." If you are not feeling confident about your future, you tend to not do certain things. When you feel confident, you tend to do certain things (i.e., shop, invest, hire, etc.) Confidence is the foundation of our whole system. If you look at our financial system, confidence is the linchpin that holds everything else up. If you pull that pin, everything collapses. We've seen this in the financial industry in particular. If you study the history of banking, for example, you will see the role that confidence plays. Even the word "credit" at its root definition means "trust." When you lend someone money, you are placing trust in that person, that they will eventually pay you back.

Why is preparedness the watchword when we are feeling confident? Because it's when we feel the strongest that we are able to bring our best thinking to the table. Let's use the snow shovel analogy. If I shop for snow shovels when I don't have immediate need for one, I have several advantages:

Expectations of results. If I run into the hardware store in December at the first snowfall, it's less likely I will have researched what is available for my needs. Sure, there might be a salesperson there to make a suggestion, but by not doing my own homework, I may not even be at the right store.

Price of choices. Retailers know they can always get a better price to satisfy an immediate need. That instant gratification would cost you if you wait too long.

Timing of decisions. Over time the best decisions are made when you've had the time to research alternatives and are able to make well-informed, intelligent decisions.

In the investment world, preparedness is critical for both clients and advisors. My experience with clients of all shapes and sizes has taught me that it's vital to set expectations from the beginning. If you set the ground rules up front, you will be far better off than springing things on clients as they come up. Remember my mentioning the heat in the summers in the desert? One of my summer strategies was to get to the coast where it was much cooler and hang out for the weekend. Sometimes this meant driving to San Diego. From the Palm Desert area of Southern California, there are two basic ways to get to San Diego by car: one via the interstate, the other via a shortcut over the San Juan Mountains. The payoff was a total time savings of at least 25 percent so I almost always opted for this route. The catch was that it was a trickier, more dangerous route. First of all, the road is windy and at times there is no shoulder between you and a steep cliff. If you happen to get stuck behind a slow driver, it might be five miles or more before you see an opportunity to make a pass. Even then, it might be dangerous because there are few high visibility pass points along the way.

If you asked for directions to get to San Diego from the desert and I gave you this route without preparing you for what to expect, you might get there, but it may cause you undue stress. Or you may decide it's just not worth the trip. It would have been far better to prepare you so you could know what to expect. Leave the surprises for novels and suspense thrillers. And it would be more effective to tell you this when your trust and confidence in me and in our relationship was at its highest. When it comes to making sound decisions, preparedness is the medicine best swallowed with the spoonful of sugar known as confidence. Imagine taking this route after my last instructions resulted in a head-on collision that nearly cost you your life! This is what happens if you don't prepare for the inevitable drops in the economy and the markets. When it comes time to make decisions, you have the least amount of trust. When you have already laid out what-if scenarios, there is a much higher likelihood of making rational choices when so much is riding on those choices.

2. Greed—Discipline

This is the stage where confidence begins to become hubris. There is usually some "asset bubble" forming. In the case of 2005–2007, it was mostly in real estate and some stocks (especially financial services companies). This is where everyone has showed up for the party and nobody is saying no at the punch bowl. It is simply irresistible not to join in on the fun. Cab drivers and manicurists have become part-time condo speculators. And nobody is ready when the pendulum swings the other way.

Why? With the real estate bubble, in hindsight the burst seems almost inevitable. Think about it. The problem with residential real estate in particular is that nobody has an incentive to say "no" to a transaction. In the old days, the bank that did the underwriting also held the loan so they "ate their own cooking." Then, when securitization came on the scene, mortgages were packaged and sold around the world to yield hungry investors in a low interest rate environment. So the loan originator had no reason to say no. As long as the music was playing they never had to worry about finding a chair.

Let's look at the other links in this greed chain. Politicians came to the conclusion that home ownership should be a right not a privilege, so they pushed banks to lend to borrowers who could not really afford to pay. Then there is the tax deduction on mortgage interest, making it seem almost stupid to pay rent if you can write off your borrowing costs. Then the real estate brokers get paid a commission when a home is bought or sold, no matter what happens down the road. The mortgage broker gets their fee at the point of funding of the loan. The developer is motivated to keep coming up with new residential developments. The builders put up more houses. All the subcontractors from the electrician to the plumber are rocking and rolling. Businesses that sell furniture, appliances, paint, fixtures, linens, etc., all do more business when households buy new homes. And you can usually get all these things with no money down. Everything can be bought on credit.

> People at the greed stage are only thinking upside
> not downside.

If you are the only one raising your hand at the party and suggesting that maybe this factor should be considered or that contingency prepared, you run the risk of being a real party-pooper. As I've alluded to earlier, social factors play a big part in how many get swept up in this phase. Your neighbor just moved out of your neighborhood into that new development. You hear stories of soaring portfolio values, early retirement of coworkers and extravagant vacations. How do you resist jumping into the water too? You can hear the chants from your friends like that frat party guy holding the beer bong saying your name over and over. What are you waiting on? You only live once. Don't be an old "fuddy-duddy."

What is the antidote in times like these? How can you shield yourself when the whole world around you seems to have "irrational exuberance?" The answer is discipline. Discipline is your primary weapon against the excesses that invariably come when greed has permeated the landscape. It's your defense against going too far, expecting too much, or losing perspective. If you learn to tap discipline at this stage you will likely save yourself a lot of grief over time. But I'll warn you, it's like fighting gravity. The pull of greed is incredibly strong. It's no wimp in the battle for your mind. When greed is in full swing, the news is so positive that you may sound like Scrooge at Christmas to suggest reigning in your risk appetite just when every stocking including your own is overflowing.

How can you show discipline? Discipline is like a muscle, you either use it or lose it. If we use discipline when things are good, it's far more likely we'll use it when things are not so good. Many people try to start diets during the holidays. Are you nuts? It would be better to show discipline prior to all the temptations rather than go cold turkey when all you see around you is turkey! It's best to have a prearranged strategy so many of these decisions become automatic, rather than require yourself to consciously go against the grain. This includes things like automatic rebalancing in a portfolio that takes the guesswork out of the equation. If a "hot sector" of the market has become too big a piece of your portfolio, this approach keeps things in check. Then this discipline forces a sell of those over-valued assets and forces a buy of under-valued assets. If you take this approach in your business or even your personal life, you avoid doing things at the extreme. Did you ever pull an all-nighter in school to complete a paper or a project? How about trying to do a budget after all your credit cards are maxed out? It's far better to plan when you are in a position of strength, not weakness, because you have more resources and alternatives to draw from. That means discipline.

3. Denial—Objectivity

Once things have peaked (which we only know in hindsight) and momentum recedes, the next phase is denial. This is when we refuse to leave the party even though the punch bowl is empty. We seem to be waiting for reinforcements—somebody to magically appear with a fresh supply of good times to keep the mood from turning down. The only cure at this stage is to take a plunge into the brisk waters of objectivity. This is best done by doing some critical thinking and asking some tough questions.

What is the reality right now? Take a serious inventory. Gather as many facts as possible about what is happening around you. Be as brutally objective as possible. What is the state of your industry, the economy, your personal finances and your portfolio?

- Looking forward, what are all the assumptions you are making about the trends you expect to continue?

- What are some of the things that could torpedo those assumptions?

- What do you need to sell right now in order to get properly diversified?

- What do you need to sell right now to maintain proper diversification?

- Are their any unfunded liabilities that you could take care of right now by selling a highly appreciated asset?

- Are you avoiding selling something because you don't want to pay taxes?

- Have you become emotionally attached to any investment?

- Has any investment become more than 15 percent of your total net worth or your portfolio?

- Which investment are you most certain will keep going up? (Let me suggest this is the one that has the most potential to go down.)

- Assuming you are wrong about a particular investment, how and when do you think you will know it?

- Is your net worth concentrated in a particular industry? Have you considered any hedging strategies to reduce your downside risk?

- Have you considered alternative investments, such as precious metals, timber, other currencies, etc.?

- What is your total debt as a percentage of net worth? How much is secured? How much is not secured?

- Have you seen bullish media coverage about an investment?

- Have you heard something positive about an investment from relatively unsophisticated sources (a stock tip from your cab driver)?

- Have you ramped up your spending based on current investment or business trends continuing?

- Have you lost patience with investments that are "out of favor"?

- Have you recently bought an investment that is considered "speculative"?

If you get the sensation that your ears are blocked, your eyes are shut and your mind is in denial, it's because your head is in the sand! The only way out is by pulling it out and figuring out where you actually are—not where you think you are or where you wish you were. That's objectivity.

4. Fear—Opportunity

Do you remember the movie *The Matrix?* The hero of the story, Neo, takes the pill and suddenly becomes aware of his horrific reality: sitting in a pod supplying energy to machines. His reality had been an elaborate computer program. When he discovers this, it's quite a scary moment. The same can be said when we emerge from feelings of denial to accept the reality of an economy and markets that are dropping like a piano falling from a tall building. We're not quite sure what it's going to sound like when it hits the ground but we're pretty sure we are not going to enjoy seeing it, or hearing it for that matter. This is the stage where irrational exuberance becomes irrational panic. The news is not just bad, it's downright depressing. We are hearing the dreaded "D" word (Depression). We brace for something we haven't seen since the 1930s. This sudden realization of impending doom repeating itself is like seeing a long forgotten crazy uncle come down from our attic. We've been hiding him so long in our minds, we've all forgotten he was still there. And under the right conditions, he can reappear to remind you.

Pass your own stimulus package. Warren Buffet said that to be a successful investor you must "be fearful when others are greedy and greedy when others are fearful." I would also add that the very factors causing the fear usually provide hidden secrets for some of the best opportunities. I say hidden because they arrive in disguise, usually as dirty pieces of coal that can become diamonds if the right pressure is applied. Here are some questions to ask that might reveal huge acres of diamonds right under your nose if you will only but look down to see them:

- What are the underlying trends, changes and adjustments that are happening in the economy and the markets right now?

- Who will see an increase in business as a result?

- What role will local, state and federal government play in solving the problem?

- Which industries and companies are best able to adapt to the new environment?

- Which industries and companies are likely to fail as a result?

- Is this a cycle issue or a longer term, systemic or structural issue?

- What are you already doing that could be beneficial in the new environment?

- Have you always wanted to start your own business? Maybe this is your chance to jump into the market with a fresh product or service.

- Which industries and companies have the financial wherewithal to take advantage of opportunities in the new environment?

- What assets are being sold below their true intrinsic value?

- How can you best reposition your assets to prepare for the next up cycle?

5. Guilt—Forgiveness

Once we've experienced fear from the drop, the next phase we must deal with is the whole aftershock of negative emotions that must be processed before we are able to move on. It's a bit like an addict going through a 12-step program. The residual toxicity is usually described as guilt, sometimes even shame. We beat up on ourselves. We engage in "should have, would have, could have" endless loop conversations with ourselves. In the movie, *The Edge,* Anthony Hopkins plays a billionaire who must survive in the wilderness after his plane goes down. He asked his fellow castaways, "What is the leading cause of death from a disaster like this?" It was a trick question because most of them were thinking that it would be a lack of fresh water, food or adequate shelter. As it turns out the answer he gave is "shame." He said folks get stuck in a pattern of toxic shame rather than focusing their energy on doing what needs to be done to survive.

It was just a movie but that line contained great wisdom—the only way to move beyond guilt is by practicing forgiveness. This may have spiritual overtones and, if it does for you, so be it. The fact is that the healing quality of forgiveness is what we all need to get beyond all the blaming and second-guessing. When we no longer blame others and the environment for our situation—when we forgive early and often—we begin to take responsibility. Forgiveness wipes the slate clean. It doesn't matter who did this or didn't do that.

It starts with forgiving yourself. As one of my coaches used to say when I made a bad play, "That's why we have erasers on our pencils." We must be ready to recover from whatever just happened and learn from it, not be imprisoned by it. Those who do not go through this forgiveness process will find themselves haunted by those negative emotions and not nearly as effective going forward in their decision-making. Here are some questions to help you move through this healing process faster:

- What lessons have you learned from any mistakes you've made?

- When you think back to prior cycles, do you find you are making the same mistakes over and over again? If so, it's time to do something differently next time.

- How are you better, stronger, smarter as a direct result of this experience?

- What did you do right when things were better?

- Did you ignore any advice that might have put you in a stronger position?

- Who are you blaming for your current situation and how can you best forgive that person?

- What environmental factors are you blaming in your situation and how can you best forgive those factors?

- Is there something else you haven't identified keeping you from forgiving yourself (an addiction, a toxic relationship, etc.)?

- What issue have you been putting off dealing with because you have not been willing to face it head on?

- What one thing could you do right now that would help you to put the past behind you and move forward?

6. Apathy—Passion

Let's return to the world of investments to shed light on this cycle. Once we move past the guilt phase and we are able to forgive from a downturn or loss, we often lose interest all together. The excitement, the adrenaline rush of confidence and the greed have long faded. Now we battle fatigue and apathy. The news is no longer as bad, it's mostly just boring.

It would be more intriguing to sit and watch paint dry than tune into what's going on with the economy or our investments. Like the laboratory rat that hits the bar without getting a food pellet, our expectations are so low we choose not to even try. After all, what's the rush?

What is the anecdote for apathy? Igniting some passion. Top advisors know this early in their careers. If you don't believe it, don't expect a client to believe it. The great actor Morgan Freeman once said that "audiences believe what you believe." The irony is that if we had to identify the best time to believe, it would be at this stage because it usually marks the very beginning of the next up leg in the economy and the markets. (Note: I'm referring to both in the same vein but the stock market usually moves up or down about six months prior to the actual economy—it's a leading indicator.)

So using the stock market as our barometer, the best time to buy is right before others do. The other advantage at this stage in the stock market cycle is that this is the point where the risk of overpaying is very low. Not only has the damage already been done, everyone knows it's been done. As we move through this stage, we see very early signs of stocks flirting with the idea of actually going up. Like a shy teenager who's been rejected a few times at the school dance, the stock market is far from showing any confidence or bold action. She's just darting glances at you from way across the room, hoping you will eventually come over and take a chance, to show your enthusiasm for her and the song playing.

Show me the love, then I'll show you the money.

So how can you find the passion to muster up the courage to get back on the economic dance floor with some enthusiasm? Look for clues in the environment. There is something in technical analysis called "relative strength" that basically says at this stage what has gone down the least will be the first to actually go up. This makes sense from a Darwinian perspective. If you were strong enough to survive the tough times, then you are even stronger when things turn up.

I used to use boat analogies to explain the stock market to clients. The market is like an ocean full of sailboats and there are times when the wind does not blow, just as there are times the economy is bad. And during those times, even the best boats aren't able to make much progress. When a storm comes, some boats will sink. That's why it's important to own quality stocks during bear markets. But you also learn a lot about your boat during those times of no wind or bad weather. This is where relative strength comes in. Some boats have crews that are working very hard when there is no wind to prepare their boat for the next race. They are figuring out their sailing strategy, making repairs, scrubbing the underbelly of the boat or becoming a more efficient team. Others are just sitting around. When the skies clear and the sails are engaged again, you can quickly separate the winners from the losers. The winners move to the lead rapidly, reflecting improvement relative to their competition.

During down times, check to see if the company stocks you own are showing their boats the love before you invest your hard-earned capital. Here are some questions you can ask to prepare for your next sail:

- Which sectors or companies have actually gotten stronger during the downturn?

- Which stocks are showing their investors the best relative strength in their stock price lately?

- What investments have been the most "boring" lately, having not moved much up or down but remained flat over an extended period of time?

- What investments are being "sold" to you right now?

- What investments seem the least sexy to you?

- What investments are getting little or no attention right now?

- Where is the majority investing their money right now?

- What seems to be the most popular investment in the news?

- Which investments seem to be no-brainer choices (hint: avoid those)?

- What can you get excited about that others don't seem to see?

7. Doubt—Trust

There is a point where even though things start looking much better, we have a hard time believing it. We're like the traveler who has been roaming the desert in search of water. We're not sure if what we're seeing is real or merely a mirage. Doubt becomes the watchword. Just when we think the coast is clear and start to cross the street, we see a car zoom past and remind us of the dangers. What we need most at this point is trust. Trust is such a basic human need that none of us would survive long without it. Think about the level of trust we show on a daily basis just with our routines. Consider what happens every day on a typical commute. Millions of cars are speeding past each other, usually within a few feet of crashing. If you travel on a two-lane road, you must appreciate the fact that one wrong move of the steering wheel and people will likely die.

I'm always been amazed by the level of trust exchanged in the financial markets on a daily basis. Phone authorization moves millions of dollars every second of every trading day. And the glue that is holding everything together is trust. The flip side is that it is a lack of trust that causes the most financial damage. It's the company that has to restate its earnings. It's the hedge fund manager who defrauded investors. At this stage, it is trust that bridges the gap between the doubt and the confidence that will come in time with the next up cycle. Those who can effectively build trust will have the most leverage, the most power to make things happen as things visibly improve. Like a guide that takes you through a dark tunnel leading to a beautiful valley on the other side, leaders and advisors who know the art of building trust have a huge competitive advantage. Here are some things you can do to help re-establish trust if you've lost your way:

- Start with small commitments
- Be consistent with your message
- Be clear with your intentions
- Offer value beyond the obvious
- Make it personal
- Be the first to offer concessions
- Find ways to help them outside business

So that's the completion of the seven cycles and how to address them. To summarize what this model can do for you, here is a simple two-step process:

1. Identify which phase you, your business, your career, your clients, your friends, your employees, etc., are in now based on the information provided. Gather additional clues by tuning in to your own emotional state and what you observe happening in your environment.

2. Implement a "counter strategy" based on what you have learned and the lessons of your own experience so you and those you influence can take advantage of these normal cycles rather than have them take advantage of you.

Remember: wealth is first and foremost a state of mind before it manifests in your outward world.

3

Naked Assets: Time to Invest in Your Own Infrastructure

I heard once that "99 percent of our assets are standing in our shoes." If that's true, then why in a bad economy do we feel like our self-worth is shrinking along with our net worth? And why do we get that sinking feeling that those shoes we're standing in had better last a lot longer because we won't be buying new shoes any time soon? Because everyone is impacted by the economy and the financial market cycles. You may even take a bad economy personally. I find this especially evident in my coaching work with financial advisors. The following illustration will give you a flavor for the stress felt among this group in particular. See if you can relate.

The morning alarm clock goes off and as you look at the time you ask yourself: How many hours' sleep did I actually get last night? Your brain goes to work calculating a number while your body longs for a return to the mattress. Then suddenly you realize you have an early-morning appointment at your office with one of your most demanding clients to review a plunging stock portfolio. After a quick shower, you put on your best "client appointment suit" while trying to listen to CNBC's *Squawk Box* blaring in the background. You glance at the television and see another clock counting down the time until the opening bell, like a horse race at Belmont. And a streaming banner declares that one of your largest client stock holdings is looking to gap down in price after just-released earnings came in below expectations. You jump into your car, wave goodbye to your family and race to your neighborhood Starbucks to wolf down a pastry along with your first cup of coffee.

So begins a typical day in the life of many advisors—often stressful, exhausting and unhealthy. Are you taking the time every day to recharge your batteries, properly manage and channel stress, eat healthy and exercise? In the best-selling book, *The Power of Full Engagement,* authors Jim Loehr and Tony Schwartz make a compelling case that managing energy, not time, is the key to high performance and personal renewal. I don't want to get off on a Jerry McGuire type rant here but many of the lifestyle habits I grew up with in the financial services industry have proven to not always be the healthiest long term. I mean there are only so many donuts, thick juicy steaks and cocktails a body can take, right? And like many things ingrained in our culture, they may taste good going down but have an insidious effect on our energy levels over time.

If you are serious about living *The Undaunted Life,* you need to learn to build and sustain the energy to do it. That means turning away from those old habits and replacing them with new ones. Here are some tools to make it happen.

7 TIPS TO BETTER MANAGE YOUR PHYSICAL ENERGY

1. Don't just burn energy, build energy capacity

To maintain our energy capacity, we must bring in intermittent energy renewal. We often hear that the world's oil supply has peaked, setting the stage for much higher prices long term. We hear that diminishing new oil discoveries, lack of refinery capacity and under-investment in alternative energy sources are a few of the culprits. Similarly, we see individuals pay a high price physically and mentally when they don't take the time to maintain and build their own energy reserves. Like the care of any engine, you have to properly maintain all the parts so you have enough horsepower when you need it. If you are not getting an annual physical, please make the commitment now to set that appointment with your doctor. Remember, early detection is the key to make sure you never have to shut down your motor for repairs—that's when the capacity needle goes to zero.

As a society we must be operating at an energy deficit most of the time because there's been an explosion in products offered to boost our energy. One could argue that Starbucks is in the caffeine delivery business. Walk into a convenience store and you'll notice a plethora of sodas with extra caffeine, and new category killers like Red Bull. Ironically, in recent years we have also seen more and more sleep disorders and medications and over-the-counter drugs to solve the problem of not being able to come down from all the caffeine. As a culture we seem to be getting more exhausted, so we engage in unhealthy ways to ramp up, only to find we get less sleep, which then leads to less energy—and the cycle continues.

2. Pay attention to the fuel that goes into your body

It's not just caffeine. There's also caffeine's evil twin brother—sugar. Often they are taken together to turbo-charge the effect (can you say Chocolate Mint Frappachino?). Processed white sugar, or high fructose corn syrup for soda fans, is one of the reasons we have a diabetes epidemic in this country. Folks turning to sugar for energy boosting will get it in the short run but will crash in the intermediate and long term. Life is a marathon with a series of sprints in between. Relying too much on sugar is like building a bigger Hummer when gas prices are skyrocketing. I drove a 1973 Cadillac El Dorado in high school and, let me tell you, it was a lot of fun to drive. But it had a gas tank like a bathtub. Whenever I hit a hill there was always a chance it would sputter out because it wasn't getting enough fuel. To make matters worse, my dad was smart enough to only give me gas money daily. Besides not wanting me to take my car on a joy ride, he also wanted to impress upon me the value of the energy I was burning to get around. When it comes to your body, you want to be much more like a Honda than a Hummer. Every pound of extra weight requires more energy to support it and when sugar is used to compensate, guess what happens? Next time it will take more sugar because the load just got heavier.

Hidden dangers of comfort food in tough times. I don't know about you, but when I'm feeling particularly stressed, there are certain foods that seem to just taste better. Maybe it has something to do with growing up in the South where comfort food is a religion. There were plenty of unhealthy choices growing up but I was presented with a dilemma early on: my mom's nickname was "the wheat-germ lady" and she was a diligent reader of *Prevention* magazine. This meant birthday cakes made with carob instead of chocolate and buckwheat pancakes with honey for breakfast. Early in my life I came to the conclusion that there are three surefire ways to make food taste good—sugar, fat and salt. When I had the occasion to stay over at a friend's home, I would get to indulge in more traditional southern fare. So what is your comfort food of choice? We have a Sunday morning tradition in our family of going to Cracker Barrel for breakfast. This fine establishment has plenty of fried, fully leaded entrees and goodies floating in a tub of butter that are sure to take my troubles away.

There is a direct connection between stress and eating. As a consequence we have to be doubly mindful of what we eat when times are tough. Some people are night grazers, some are all-day snackers and some are binge eaters. And some love fast food. As Jimmy Buffet reminds us, there is a "cheeseburger in paradise." Many folks feel compelled to hit the drive-through to save time in our rushed culture. True, it will take time to find alternatives, but it will save you much wear and tear in the long term. We recently had a Whole Foods store come to town and for less than many fast food meals, I can enjoy their freshly prepared buffet of garden fresh, nutrient rich alternatives. Scout out these types of places in your area and insist on avoiding processed white flour, white sugar, high fructose corn syrup, hydrogenated oils (trans fats), too much saturated fat, preservatives and artificial coloring. Instead, focus on foods that are rich in colors and low in sugar and fat.

There are many "stealth calories" that can add up during the day. One of the most deadly sources is soda. Within the next 24 hours, go out and buy a supply of fresh water for your office. And for the next 30 days, instead of drinking sodas, try drinking that water throughout the day.

Here's a factoid from the book *You: Staying Young* by Michael F. Roizen. Did you think that just because diet sodas are calorie-free that they are also "guilt-free" too? Sorry. Even drinking diet drinks is associated with a higher risk of metabolic-syndrome (diabetes). Consumption of sugar (or its equivalent, such as corn syrup) in soft drinks has been linked to obesity in children and adolescents in research studies. One theory is that the high sweetness of drinks conditions people to crave sweet foods. Another is that ingredients in the drinks can lead to insulin resistance or inflammation.

Also, be careful of that second cup of java—while caffeine has been proven to improve mental awareness and retention, too much can be a problem. Limit caffeine intake to modest portions three times per day (morning, midday, afternoon). Avoid after 6:00 p.m. to allow evening wind down and prepare for sleep. Just say no to snack foods that spike your blood sugar. Avoid simple processed sugars like candy. Try eating an apple or other natural snack with more complex carbohydrates instead. In times of stress, fries, milk shakes or your grandmother's bread pudding can offer comfort. But just because Warren Buffet gets away with eating that stuff doesn't mean you can. Wouldn't it be great if drinking fully leaded colas and milk shakes from Dairy Queen also increased our net worth? Many nutritionists recommend eating smaller portions four times a day rather than three larger meals. And one trick that works to curb nighttime sugar cravings is to immediately brush your teeth after your evening meal.

Whatever your brand of indulgence, keep your radar up to detect when you are most likely to feel stressed and come up with ways to avoid using food as your drug of choice to ease your pain.

3. Get the right quantity and quality of rest

Are you consistently getting seven to eight hours of sleep a night? Experts say that's the number for the body and mind to properly recover and remain healthy. Checking stock prices over the Internet before bedtime promotes busy mindedness and makes it harder to slip into deep, restful sleep. Many find that taking a hot bath or reading just prior to bedtime works wonders. Some find that keeping a journal next to their bed allows them to vent on paper, thus transferring some of the stress of the day onto the page instead of swirling around in your head. Creative work favors the relaxed mind, so if you have a pressing issue requiring out-of-the-box thinking, a calm night's sleep can become a powerful tool as well. It's also better to have the room as dark as possible to promote deep sleep. I recall once living in a condo where I had to use shutout-type blinds to block a parking lot light that seemed to penetrate even the most hearty window shades.

Noise is an underrated factor when it comes to getting a good night's rest. Though some find that a steady noise is fine, random noise coming from such distractions as traffic, horns, voices, etc., can make evenings seem like mental jousting matches with a series of noise opponents popping up just when the last one seems to have faded. I've encountered this before my speaking engagements where slamming doors can break even the deepest rest. Where possible, I'll request a room as far from other guests as possible.

Your energy and the laws of physics. It's also true that there are people who perhaps sleep too much. Sloth is one of the seven deadly sins for a reason. Too much rest leads to energy leakage. It's like a car that is not driven—soon parts begin to rust from inactivity. There are laws of physics here at play. You may remember from your high school physics class that "a body in motion tends to stay in motion" and "a body that is not in motion will stay that way until acted upon with an external force." Most psychologists agree that it's better to "act your way into feeling than it is to try to feel your way into acting." There is a message that your body gets when you are moving—something is happening—and it tends to reinforce a more positive self-image. One of my favorite sayings is that "it's not what you say you are going to do; the only thing that counts is what you are actually doing." We will discuss the power of momentum in a later chapter but the fact is that getting started on any new course of action is half the battle. This action orientation is even more important when the environment seems most unclear.

Act boldly and unseen forces will come to your aid.

The root word in "emotion" is "motion." The more energy we put towards something the more emotion we derive from that activity. And the more emotion we derive, the more psychic energy goes back into our physical bodies and a virtuous cycle emerges. Have you ever heard the expression "if you want something done, give it to a busy person?"

The power of inner thoughts. There's one more point related to energy. Though not directly linked to the topic of rest, I want to briefly touch upon it before moving on to the fourth tip to better manage your physical energy. The point is that it's also important to recognize how our inner thoughts manifest in our outer reality and life experience. We are all made up of subatomic particles that are part of a much larger universe. Obviously we don't understand all the ways this works, but I can tell you from my own experience and from studying success for many years, we have vast amounts of untapped human potential. And we can dramatically boost our energy levels by understanding the link between our thoughts and how movement creates its own power of attraction. When we visualize what we want and focus our energy there, the laws of physics begin to shape our outer world to reflect that image.

What is lacking in this concept, in my opinion, is that there must also be massive action. Picture a turbine. When that turbine is still, there is massive potential energy but no electricity is generated until that turbine is forced to move—to rotate faster and faster until the laws of physics creates that current and power is flowing smoothly toward its destination. It's the same with our bodies. When we are moving, we in effect become magnetized. We accelerate our attraction power to bring in the things, people and circumstances to make our desires our reality. When it comes to maintaining high levels of vitality, especially in times of high stress, the mantra should be "use it or lose it."

4. Practice dee-ee-ee-ee-p breathing

There is good reason why someone might recommend that you take a deep breath when you're upset or stressed out about something. Deep breathing is the best way to increase nitric oxide to help your lungs and blood vessels open up better and function more efficiently. Most of us discount how important is the act of simply breathing to how our engines run. If you've ever tried to stoke a fire, you know that oxygen is essential to both starting and maintaining it. If you choke off the oxygen, the fire dies.

Remember that our breathing is one of the essential ways our bodies take out the trash. So you can imagine what is happening inside you if the garbage is left to fester with each little breath. Because our breathing happens automatically, we don't have to give our bodies conscious instructions, but posture is key when it comes to getting the most benefit of each breath. Our mothers told us to "stand up straight" also for good reason. It turns out that good posture leads to better breathing. When we throw our shoulders back, it allows our diaphragm muscle to expand much larger and thus to pull in more vital oxygen. If you slump your shoulders, it's likely you are denying your body those critical incremental amounts of oxygen that keep that well-tuned machine cranking and your waste disposal mechanism working properly. Also, as strange as it seems, the act of yawning is quite healthy as it rushes oxygen into the body and it's usually an indication that we've been constricted in our posture. We associate yawning with being tired but it's also a sign that we need to get moving to avoid further fatigue.

5. Incorporate aerobic fitness and strength training

When you are going through tough times, you need to have the stamina not to fold under all the pressure. And I know of no better single stress reducer than doing something to break a sweat. I for one could not imagine not being physically fit—there is just no way we will ever be able to do what we want to do in our lives if we are not in shape physically. In order to contribute meaningfully we first need to have a spring in our step. For those looking to develop a minimum level of aerobic fitness to build your lung capacity and endurance (as opposed to running a marathon), try starting the day with a 30-minute brisk walk. Going back to the laws of physics, if you can get yourself moving physically, it is far easier to get moving mentally, emotionally and professionally. When we do any type of aerobic exercise, such as walking or a stairmaster machine, we kick into gear our whole body as a living system.

First, we are contracting muscles. This has a dual benefit as we not only burn calories but also stimulate our lymphatic system, which is believed to help prevent disease. Of course, our most important muscle of all is the heart. There was a time in our history when exercise was viewed with suspicion because it was believed we only had a certain number of heartbeats in us and if we exceeded that number our heart would stop beating. Now we know better. It's clear that not only do people who are physically active live longer, their quality of life is better. They are able to do things longer and maintain a much more active lifestyle. My dad has always been a serious walker. As a kid it was a challenge just keeping up with him. Now he's in his mid-80s and I can tell you that walking is one of the reasons he's so healthy. You really see the difference in lifestyle when you watch people get into their 70s and 80s. Folks who retire to a rocking chair lose energy capacity fast. Those who maintain even a modest walking regimen have far higher levels of energy than those that don't.

If you are able to combine aerobic fitness with other interests, all the better. Hiking is a perfect example. You can create an entire vacation around daily hiking. Even in previously sedentary venues, you'll find more of an emphasis on movement. For example, cruise ships now offer many more amenities for more active passengers, including very sophisticated gyms, rock climbing walls and aerobics classes.

Whatever you decide upon as your exercise routine, make sure to include abdominal training. Terms like "core training" describe how various exercises use the muscles in and around your midsection to provide a strong foundation for everything else that you do. That's why it's called "core." When the back and stomach muscles are strong and healthy, it dramatically enhances your ability to do a variety of physical activities.

There is also a discipline aspect to exercise that plays out over time. Invariably, those who are able to discipline themselves to exercise demonstrate discipline in other areas as well. For example, concentration levels are higher among those whose fitness levels are higher. The higher flow of oxygen to their bodies also means they get more oxygen to their brains. The link can be seen in the game of golf. If you watch someone like a John Daly live, you might conclude that golf is not a game requiring much stamina. But nothing could be further from the truth. There is a reason Tiger Woods works out and is in incredible shape. It gives him an edge when the match becomes a marathon tie-breaker. The stronger he is, the more control he has of his swing and his mind.

Most people underestimate the importance of this dimension of overall life success. Without a healthy physical body, without the vitality necessary to do things, all the other stuff is just conversation. I'm always amazed to hear people talk about planning retirement, then go outside to light up a cigarette. What do you think is going to happen in those later years? Making all the right moves in your career, your investments, your relationships will all be trumped by the deterioration of your physical body.

There have been numerous studies done with senior citizens that hit the weight room and discover the link between strength training and overall health. Gone are the days that you had to be an Arnold Schwarzenegger shouting out "no pain, no gain" in mirror-lined, steroid-pumping gyms. There is no need to get masochistic about using basic resistance training to gain strength.

Flexibility. As we age, our muscles tend to become less elastic. Having been a personal trainer at a gym, I've seen very strong guys become frustrated when they seem to be stuck at a certain strength level. The one thing they can do to make a dramatic difference in performance is to get aggressive about stretching those big muscles out. Only then can they hope to recondition the muscle to accommodate a higher weight. The lesson I learned is that flexibility is every bit as important as aerobic and strength fitness. When flexibility is combined with aerobic fitness and strength training, you have a trifecta of energy-enhancing tools at your disposal. Assuming you are not training for an Olympic event, there are some basic stretching exercises that can make a big difference.

One measure of flexibility is to simply stand with your feet shoulder width apart and try to touch your toes without bending your knees. How far can you go? Other forms of exercise and movement also can be helpful. Chi gong, for example, is a set of ancient body movements that strengthen the immune system, reduce stress and improve balance and posture.

Prevent defense. Coaches always taught me that defense was more important than offense, so you want your best athletes to be on defense. The premise was simple: in order to win we must first not lose. As we age, the name of the game is prevention, or what I call "prevent defense." The best athletes in any sport are players who successfully anticipate what will happen next and make moves now to be in the best position. The "great one," Wayne Gretzky, was known for saying that the secret was not looking at the puck but anticipating where the puck was going to be and skating ahead of it. Baseball players get paid big bucks for reading a pitch as it's released from a pitcher's hand. The best rebounders in basketball can tell you where the ball is going to go by seeing the rotation on the ball before it even gets near the basket. So it is with surviving tough times by building your energy capacity.

6. Pay attention to your body's signals

There is nothing more tragic than to hear stories about how somebody felt something wrong but never bothered to seek a professional diagnosis. Our bodies have remarkable healing powers but they need your help to operate in an optimum fashion. For example, if you are a man over 40 you need to get an annual checkup, which will include blood work and prostate check. If you are a woman, periodic breast exams are a must. High blood pressure, diabetes, cancer—all these top killers are best detected early in the game. For example, the vast majority of men will have some form of prostate cancer, and early treatments tend to be highly successful. We all know women who have suffered from breast cancer, and the earlier the diagnosis the greater the odds of survival.

Turn stress into fuel. There is a fine line between being energized and excited about something and having that same situation become a real downer. Learn to recognize that there is good stress and bad stress and much of it depends on how we interpret what is happening. When you are faced with a stressful situation, what is going through your mind? What emotions are you feeling? Ask yourself if what you are feeling can be turned into fuel for progress rather than stress that debilitates. For example, if you have been fired from a job, can you turn that feeling of anger into motivation to get an even better job? Michael Jordan used to "save up insults" during the off-season to amp up his motivation during the season. Often we internalize things that with a little adjustment in interpretation can be made to empower rather than victimize you.

Ask yourself if perhaps your stress is self-induced. Once I can remember being stressed out about something a client told me in passing about their investment portfolio. For some reason, I interpreted that as an imminent sign that they were leaving me. It turns out it was actually the opposite. What they were looking for was advice on how to steer a friend clear of an investment they suspected was too risky. If only I had probed sooner—instead I took a leap of "dis-faith" and decided to lose sleep over it.

We can use stress to identify areas of opportunity by learning to ask ourselves and others, "Where does it hurt?" If you are having a particular problem causing you stress, consider how it might be a signal that there are others with the same issue, thus emerges an opportunity.

7. Develop rituals that make the right things to do the easy things to do

The key to any exercise program is to make it as routine as possible. That means doing it in the same location at the same time every day so that it's as natural as brushing your teeth. You know you've got it right when you actually forget you did it afterwards. (Note: this does not apply to all areas of physical exertion or if you are eligible for social security and have a family history of dementia!)

Every aspect of managing your energy can be improved if you develop the right rituals. Here are some energy-enhancing rituals that can make a big difference.

Select a grocery store such as Whole Foods where you know they have done some of the nutritional homework for you and can save you time. For example, if you are trying to avoid trans fats, they simply don't sell products with trans fats so you don't have to waste time worrying about it. They also have excellent produce and helpful staff so you can create more nutritious meals. They even have to-go meals that you can assemble at the store quickly.

Consider converting space in your home to make a home gym. There are many companies that sell home fitness equipment. When going to work out is as simple as walking down the hall, you are more likely to do it.

Keep a supply of fresh water at work. Also, anticipate being hungry for snacks and bring a piece of fruit such as an apple to work instead of other less healthy snacks.

Avoid eating while watching television. The habit of eating in front of the TV can lead to a kind of zoning out where you'll end up eating more than you realize. If you choose to drink, be aware that we all generally eat more when we drink.

Allow wind-down time between work and home. It's good to have a transition time between home and the office. Otherwise it's harder to put on your other hats for your other roles in life such as parent and spouse.

Remember: "Wherever you are, be there." I was told this many years ago. One sure way to drain energy is to be somewhere physically but elsewhere mentally. This goes for all you BlackBerry users. People you care about want your full, undivided attention.

Frequent restaurants where you know ahead of time how you will order to reach your dietary goals. Nothing like looking at a menu for the first time only to discover that nothing really fits your guidelines and you revert to something along the lines of comfort food.

As you expand your energy capacity, other areas will naturally expand by extension, such as your income.

4 TIPS TO EXPAND YOUR EARNINGS POTENTIAL

It's not where you are, it's where you are going. Have you ever encountered someone along your life's path where you said to yourself "that person's going somewhere" or "I'd love to have this person on my team?" Have you also had a service experience where you thought "there's no way that person is ever going to move up" or asked "how does that person even keep their job?" In all my years of interviewing and hiring financial advisors it was amazing to see how few ever really took the time to understand what it was going to take to be successful and exactly what they were going to have to do to make it. The best always knew where they were going and how they saw themselves getting there. When others see you as somebody "going somewhere," don't be surprised to see them come to your aid to help you. But if you don't know where you are going, don't be surprised if nobody helps you. It's not maliciousness, just reality.

And where you're going may mean giving up things you have now. I firmly believe that:

> If you are not willing to give up what you have to get what you want, you better hang on tight because that is all you are going to get.

That may mean starting a new business or launching a new career. It will likely mean leaving your comfort zone. You will likely make many mistakes on your new path and that is not only OK, it's essential. If you show me a person who hasn't made many mistakes, I'll show you someone who hasn't attempted much. Usually the biggest successes come from those who have also experienced the greatest failures. So if you are looking for a job and don't have a track record of success, don't be overly concerned about where you start. Just get moving forward in the right direction. And be ready, willing and able to make mistakes along the way. Focus more on being around what you would ultimately like to be doing not just on the work you will start out doing. Ask yourself if the next step moves you in the right direction as opposed to whether the next step gets you there in one move. Success is not about one move—it's about a series of moves all going in the direction you want to go. As Al Berstein the boxing analyst use to say:

"Success often begins with a mis-step in the right direction."

1. Don't be afraid to start at the bottom

Please know that there is no shame in starting at the bottom. In fact, you will often learn much more starting there than anywhere else. You also will have a much better opportunity to put together a success track record because it's easier to impress when expectations are low. One of the reasons I've always been a fan of the frontlines for rapid learning is the immediate feedback. In sports, you can draw it on a blackboard all day long, but until you test it on the playing field with real competitors, it's just an academic exercise.

If you have ever been snow skiing, you know that there is a counter-intuitive link between speed and control. The irony is that you have more control when your skis and your body are pointing out over the hill and you are moving than when you are tentative with your weight on the back of your skis and moving slowly. If you can visualize being at the bottom of the hill you will get there. At the same time, what happens if you start thinking about falling? That's usually when you hit the ground—smack! As you climb that ladder of success, don't waste time looking down.

2. Always have a bigger agenda

When you study successful people, you will discover that one "best practice" is to always have a bigger agenda, a larger vision for how what you are doing now is preparing you for something more significant. I love watching *A&E Biography* because you learn things about people that you might not otherwise discover. For example, I remember seeing a special on the life of Sonny Bono, who died in a tragic ski accident. We all know about Sonny and Cher but did you know how Sonny started his career? He drove a delivery truck in the Hollywood area but his "bigger agenda" was getting into the music business. In between deliveries he would call on music industry executives. Sometimes he would pitch a song he had written; other times he would try to get a job at a studio. Ultimately, he landed an entry-level job in the mailroom. There he had the chance to interact with important people at all levels of the company. After proving himself, he was offered a promotion and later would meet Cher and develop a singing act. The rest, as they say, is history.

Know this: it's very rare that somebody pulls you aside and gives you this bigger agenda. Most people don't think big anyway. When I was in the ninth grade playing the saxophone in the marching band, nobody pulled me aside and said, "Hey, if you quit the band to play football, you will be much more successful." I was always intrigued by the story that Howard Hughes took a job as a baggage handler to learn about the airline industry. You need to face the fact that people in your environment have a full plate just worrying about their own future, much less how they can help yours. If you are in a situation where you know you can be more and do more, make sure to map out a strategy to find ways to showcase your talents. Don't wait on someone else or the right circumstances.

3. Be a learning machine

Warren Buffet is known for his investment prowess, but did you also know that his longtime business partner describes him as "a learning machine?" One of the things you will find in all highly successful people is a thirst for knowledge. They maintain a childlike curiosity about things they don't yet know and since there is an unlimited supply of things to learn and things to discover, opportunities abound to expand your mind and your earnings. Here is a billionaire many times over still learning as he approaches 80. Wow, talk about teaching an old dog new tricks. It's kind of like seeing a person running who is thin and concluding, "Oh, they don't need to run. Look at them—they are already thin!" Upon further reflection, though, we realize that they are thin because they are running.

It's likely that this quality of lifetime learning will result in a boost to your lifetime earnings, not just allow you to be a winning contestant on a game show. Here are some strategies for how to translate learning more into earning more.

Read books. I once read that "leaders are readers." There is so much valuable knowledge to learn from books (both fiction and nonfiction). Make the commitment to read at least 20 to 30 minutes each day in your field and you will advance more rapidly than you can presently imagine. Part of the secret in reading is what happens while you read. It brings mental focus to bear and consequently adds fuel to your fire. For example, let's say that you are in sales of some kind and you are reading a book where you learn about a new strategy implemented by company XYZ. You think to yourself, "Wow, what if somebody did that in our industry?" You approach key decision-makers at your company and soon your suggestion is adopted, leading to your promotion. All because of something you read. In our attention-deficit-disorder culture, few people actually read entire books anymore. Do you get your information just from TV or the Internet? We seem to be inundated with sound bites and, like ordering that burger and fries through the drive-through, we get a steady diet of bad calories. It's like eating a jelly donut—it tastes good going down but has zero nutritional value. Good books, on the other hand, are loaded with nutrient rich material that expand our minds and our value.

Read quality periodicals. There is value in some periodicals like magazines and newspapers; you just have to be choosy. Mainstream media publications have frankly become more titillating than stimulating, so focus more on substance than flashy packaging. Here's a clue: if the picture-to-word space ratio is greater than two-to-one, you are probably in for a "dumbed down" reading. And, where possible, avoid blatant editorial bias.

Listen to learning CDs in your car. When I was new to the brokerage business, audio tapes accelerated my skill development much more than any formal training. We spend a huge amount of time in our society commuting. Turn driving time into learning time by using CDs. There are a wide variety of materials available on a vast range of topics.

Instead of listening to all the bad news about the economy, try listening to a motivational or inspirational message instead. This can make a real difference in your attitude as you begin to focus your attention on solutions rather than problems, and as you begin to think about challenges as opportunities.

Attend workshops in your field. As you assume responsibility for your own education, take advantage of seminars and workshops in your area that can really turbo-charge your learning efforts. There is nothing like a live event experience to act as a catalyst to change and progress. One of the hidden benefits of attending workshops and seminars is the people you meet and the contacts you make. Have you ever been to a live concert? There is something about seeing material delivered at a live event that takes everything to another level. We can all learn something new—we just have to be willing to open our minds. You also have the chance to gain some perspective because you are away from all the distractions at work. Imagine what you can learn if you are not on the phone or getting interrupted.

Consider getting advanced education. In today's job market, you can bet that advanced education will give you an edge if you know how it applies to what you are trying to do. There are many fields such as medicine and law where getting advanced education is not even an option, it's a must. But the question is: Will it help if I have an MBA? My answer is that it all depends. I don't think an MBA will ever be a substitute for actual work experience. But if I were just starting out, I would strongly consider it but would not go into deep debt to get it. A better approach might be to see if a prospective employer offers tuition reimbursement. That way you can have it financed and at the same time not have to leave your day job. It also depends on your family situation. Is it really worth having your face buried in books when you end up missing those precious years of child raising, for example? One of the motivators for me not pursuing an advanced degree at this point in my life is I want to be there for my kids.

4. Nurture your relationships

The Bible says, "What really does a man gain, if he gains the world but loses his soul?" To me this means that we have to pay attention to what is most important. That means nurturing our relationships. When we look back on our lives, it's the relationships we'll most treasure, not the extra time we put in at the office. So let's talk about how to invest in your relationship infrastructure.

Family. More and more companies are realizing that policies that put family first end up putting the company itself way ahead of the competition. Start by developing a vision for all your family roles. For example, as a father I want my wife and kids to see that they come first. And the way I demonstrate that is to be engaged at the one-on-one level on a daily basis. There are no shortcuts here either as far as time commitment. As Steven Covey says, "Things fast, people slow." Like a fine wine, relationships, starting with family, take time to nurture and develop. The good news is that the payoff can be huge. Ask yourself the hard question: What if I don't put in the time? When it comes to our legacy, for most of us that means our kids. How can you be truly successful if you make millions but your children don't really know you and you surely don't know them?

We see more and more "fly-by" parenting where we spend only a few minutes a day and sometimes less. Then we wonder why our kids are having trouble in school or with friends. Show them they are valuable by giving them something only you can give—your full undivided attention. There are so many parents that need to listen to that Harry Chapin song "Cat's in the Cradle." We've battled the role of TV in our household because it's such an easy crutch when my wife and I need to talk. But when you rely on TV as a pacifier, you miss so many awesome moments to teach and lead kids.

Friends. When I was a kid growing up, making friends seemed so easy. I had a great neighborhood full of kids my age. Then there was my school where we all had something in common and were forced together every day. Ah, the good old days. . . . But the reality is that as adults we tend not to invest in friendships as much as we should. I had a great aunt who lived to be 107 years old. When I first met her she was only 75 but she looked and acted 25 years younger. She lived in San Diego and I remember my family taking a cross-country trip that included a two-day stay with her. I will never forget the afternoon we arrived. She took us down to the beach where we discovered that the sand was extraordinarily hot. The temperature was probably in the low 90s because of the ocean breeze but the sun was just baking all that white sand. We had taken our shoes off and were all making our way to the crashing ocean waves when we suddenly all stopped, turned to each other and without saying another word started running toward the sidewalk that was bordered by a two-foot high stone wall. What we saw next is the topic of family conversations to this day. Our 75-year-old aunt was running faster than all of us, leading the way off that beach. And when she reached the stone wall, she hurdled it like an Olympian track star, carrying her purse like a baton.

She was "really cool" to us not just because she lived in southern California but because she defied every stereotype regarding age. She was like a movie star. Everywhere we went, people seemed to come out of the woodwork to talk with her. She knew everybody and she considered them all "friends." She had cards and letters from friends around the world, and she would get phone calls all day long. She would get party invitations as well as be asked to go to dinner and lunch. And, boy, could she tell great stories and funny jokes. She ultimately outlived two husbands (the second was 15 years her junior) and was quite lucid up until her death. I remember her saying to us on that trip:

"Friends are so important. They keep me young at heart."

Our rushed lives seem to leave less and less time for friends, yet it's in having friends where much of our joy will come. Take the time to invest in your friendships. It's a guaranteed return and will build something that can last a lifetime.

Coworkers. Most of us spend more time at work than anyplace else, yet we tend to discount the value of relationships with our coworkers and others in our field. When I used to recruit financial advisors from competing firms, one of the things I did was find out who they might already know in my branch. Invariably, if there was someone considered a "friend" in my branch, I had an edge. This also can have the opposite impact if you are not careful. Just like having people you like at work can enhance the quality of your life, having someone you can't stand can have a deleterious effect over time as well. The key with colleague relationships is to identify those whom you enjoy being around and, as much as possible, avoid those you don't. If you are unfortunate enough to have to work with somebody who really gets on your nerves, realize that you have control over how you are reacting to this person. When I worked in a home-office environment, there was a huge political component to getting ahead. I was once pulled aside and told that "95 percent of your success here will be political." While I don't agree with all the ramifications of that statement, I found it nonetheless true. The fact is that time you spend nurturing relationships with coworkers will pay huge dividends. This is especially vital in working teams. I've witnessed first hand what happens after a team spends time together at a retreat, for example. By spending time getting to know each other outside of their regular interaction, new relationship dynamics emerge that can dramatically impact bottom-line productivity. Team members say things like, "Oh, that's why so and so does that or doesn't do that. . . ." When you can get a breakthrough with colleagues it's truly amazing how an entire department can come alive with newfound purpose and commitment to each other.

Bosses. It's been said that your choice of a boss will either make or break your career (even if that boss is yourself, if you are considering going into business yourself). There is nothing quite as stressful as working with a boss you don't like and, even worse, you don't respect. But I think it's vital to distinguish between a "bad boss" and one that is asking you to do things you don't like to do. A bad boss in the purest definition is someone who lacks true leadership ability. As for doing things you don't like, the question becomes how much of your day is spent doing those things versus other things you do like. If you are a boss, let's take a look at what you should be doing.

Listen for understanding: This is such a basic skill but the deepest human need is to be understood. If you are a boss and the people who report to you feel you don't understand where they are coming from, you will have problems. Have regular one-on-one time. When you establish a routine of always placing time on the calendar for getting together with those who report directly to you, you allow for many problems to be resolved before they can fester and do real harm.

Communicate vision: Everyone should know where you are taking the ship and why. Everyone should clearly understand the role they play in getting it there. Silos where folks don't know what others do can sabotage success and be an extremely inefficient use of resources.

Delegate, then focus on results: Nobody, and I mean nobody, likes to work for someone breathing down their necks. Individuals should be allowed to solve problems in their own way to get the desired results. Bosses should decide ahead of time whether a person is the right person for the job, then get out of the way and let them succeed.

As an employee, here are some tips to help you nurture your relationship with your boss.

Don't assume things: Just because someone is a boss, don't assume they know everything they should about what is happening around you and them. If there is something you see that could damage or help the vision as it's laid out, somebody has to say something and that person is you since you already have energy on the subject given that you even noticed it.

Know the bottom line: If you surveyed a group of bosses and asked them the qualities they are seeking, right at the top would be the ability to know the bottom line. You always need to know "what success looks like" in any project. If you don't know what it looks like, how can anyone determine whether it's been achieved? Usually the 80–20 rule applies. Out of 10 tasks, 80 percent of the bottom-line value will be with 20 percent of the tasks. So guess where you should devote 80 percent of your time?

Speed counts: There is no better way to advance than to become known as a go-to person in a particular area and to get things done with alacrity. In our fast-paced economy, speed rules and, with all the technology tools available, those who can deliver on a deadline have a huge advantage over those who are driving in the slow lane at work.

Bosses are human too: Always keep in mind that bosses are people first. And it can be very lonely being the boss. Whenever possible, make sure you don't fall into the trap of gossiping at the water cooler about your boss or succumbing to peer pressure about "sucking up too much." Bosses need to know that they can trust those who report to them and, if you are the first one to run off and stab them in the back, believe me, eventually word gets back around. I always learned to watch out for "passive aggressive" types when I was a boss. These are the people who say one thing to your face but are the first to speak negatively about new initiatives behind your back.

Community. Let's start with our neighbors. Here's a short quiz: Do you know the first and last names of all the neighbors on your street? How about the names of all their kids? Their pets? Do you know what each of your neighbors does professionally? Do you know where they work? How about their hobbies and interests? One sign of the times is that many of us don't know our neighbors, or at least don't know them as well as we should. In a culture that seems to be more and more counting on the government to take care of our communities, this sense of community doesn't get the attention it deserves. If the art of conversation has given way to text messaging, the art of being neighborly has given way to building bigger fences. There are so many hidden resources locked away in communities. When I was growing up, it was common to find many of the kids in the neighborhood at different houses. There was a feeling of safety and security when we roamed beyond our yard because my parents knew their parents and so it went all around our development. I remember not being able to get away with much because you could count on another mom or dad to be on watch and not hesitate to pick up the phone to report something amiss.

One of the unseen benefits of hard times is a return to some old-fashioned values when it comes to rediscovering our communities. After all, if you happen to be out of work, you might finally reconnect with that neighbor you've been waving at for so many years but never bothered to get to know.

HUMOR: THE UNIVERSAL SALVE

I once had the good fortune of running into one of my favorite political figures in recent history—retired U.S. Senator Allan Simpson of Wyoming. He was to speak at a gathering and I was able to corner him in a restaurant lobby and strike up a conversation. As we discussed the book he had just written about his experience in the rough-and-tumble world of politics, he told me that having a sense of humor was critical to his surviving this "contact sport." He said that his mother taught him growing up that "humor is the universal salve that soothes all of life's abrasions." Have you noticed in everyday life that having a sense of humor when things don't go as planned can make all the difference in how quickly you recover? Are you old enough to remember the video game *Asteroids?* Remember how there was a button you could push that would create a temporary "force field" around your spaceship to protect you from the oncoming asteroids? Humor does the same thing by creating a protective layer to our psyche, empowering us to deflect things that could be harmful if allowed to enter our orbit. And in tough times, there is no shortage of the daily bombardment that can come from a variety of sources.

Customers and clients need humor too, especially in bad times. I know that in the financial services arena humor can be tricky because advising people about their money is serious business. But the best doctors have a sense of humor even when dealing with life-or-death illness, so why can't the rest of us? Do you ever think that maybe sometimes we are taking ourselves too seriously? Take the world of investment professionals. The media often views them as being in a "stuffy" or "greedy" profession. Have you seen those TV ads from discount brokers that show guys in high-back leather chairs who remind you of Mr. Potter in the movie classic *It's a Wonderful Life?* It's that stern, older condescending Daddy Warbucks-type look.

Once when I was a branch manager of a major brokerage firm, I attended a meeting with other managers where they had a professional humorist speak. Afterwards, many said it was the best session they had ever attended as a manager. Picture a group of 100 managers, mostly men, seated in orderly rows of chairs, wearing dark suits and white shirts. Now imagine that same group being told that we were dying of "terminal seriousness" and the only cure was to perform a clown-like "bat face" involving facial and hand contortions, while jumping up and down on one leg. Wow, it was something to behold. That humorist shared with us a gripping story about a pilot who had to fly a plane after its top had been blown off and the engines were failing. Incredibly, he was able to safely land the plane with no casualties. But when they listened to the cockpit recording of the ordeal, people were amazed at how this pilot was joking the entire time, making fun of himself and getting others around him to laugh. Humor really is one of our strongest innate defense mechanisms to ward off disaster under pressure—some say even to prevent disease!

Consider how humor can dramatically increase your sales and client satisfaction. For example, research shows that "chemistry" is the number one factor in clients choosing a financial advisor. Not track record or range of services, but chemistry. Can you think of a better way to demonstrate chemistry with someone than sharing a laugh?

Here are three everyday tips to help you take your job seriously but not yourself.

Smile. Smiling puts everyone in your world at ease and is the universal signal that the other person is accepted in any situation. It draws people in and it's far easier to laugh and experience the miracle quality of humor and laughter if we're already doing the next best thing. In the famous book, *How to Win Friends and Influence People,* Andrew Carnegie talks about the power of a genuine smile to transform lives and attract people to you. It's the secret of many top performers in different fields where people skills are required. And it's one of those things that comes right back to reward you immediately, a guaranteed return on investment. If you smile at others they will reciprocate.

Belly laugh at least once per day. Have you ever experienced one of those laughs where you find yourself leaning forward, your face lights up, you lose all self-consciousness and you feel a rhythmic sort of shake in your belly? There may be nothing better, even . . . well, maybe not that, but you get the point. And it's infectious—everyone around you starts to laugh and they may not even know why. It's like an injection of fresh air into a stuffy room. It just feels refreshing, invigorating. All is now right with the world. Laughing also lowers blood pressure, increases oxygen in the blood and reduces stress.

Surround yourself with people who like to laugh. I have an advisor friend who has a boisterous laugh that sometimes can be a bit loud. But if you are ever feeling down, he's someone you just want to hang around because he doesn't seem to be taking life as seriously as the rest of us. That's a joy, especially when it's raining cats, dogs and other large mammals right on your head! Even better, look to become someone like that to be a beacon of light for others.

When you think about your "Naked Assets," remember the magic of humor. It can brighten your day and be the "universal salve that soothes all of life's abrasions."

4

Pull Now™: How to Unleash Your Inner Hero

Imagine that you are a captain of a great ship back in the age of explorers in the 16th century. You have been asked to discover a new route to greatly accelerate trade between your country and a far-off land. How will you select your crew? What will be your strategy to get the most out of that crew? How will you best map your route? What tools will you need? What will be the keys to success on this voyage? Why should someone volunteer to sail with you on such a dangerous adventure?

As it turns out, you were extraordinarily successful in your adventure and everyone involved became a hero in the process. How did this happen? In hindsight, you were the perfect choice as leader because you got to know your crew better than they knew themselves. That was the critical ingredient in your success. You knew the strengths and weaknesses of each crew member. You knew their talents and abilities. You took the time to understand what drove each of them, based not on extrinsic rewards and punishments but on intrinsic forces. You discovered the secret to bringing out the best in yourself and others in challenging times.

This chapter is about tapping resources inside you that you may not even know exist. It's about finding ways to unleash your inner hero and the inner hero of those around you—a key component of living *The Undaunted Life*.

Have you ever found yourself so completely immersed in a work activity that you completely lost track of time? Have you experienced moments of unbridled joy from doing something for someone else?

Have you thought about what you would do if you won the lottery? How about if you found out you only had six months to live? When you are gone from this earth, what do you want to have said about you? What I'm describing is what I call Pull. I want to get right to the core of why we are drawn to some things and not to others. And I want to draw a contrast between being "pushed" to do something and being "pulled" or compelled to do something. Pull is that magical force within us all that once tapped cannot be denied. It is a force that is unstoppable.

When we are pushed into something, we feel manipulated, out of control, forced against our will. This state is a major de-motivator. In contrast, when we tap into pull power we are briskly pulled along a path that we are effortlessly compelled to take. We become part of something greater than ourselves. Like a magnet, we are inexplicably attracted to a vision that propels us forward. We are truly going with the flow. We are doing things "on purpose." There is choice-less awareness in that all our decisions are made at a gut level—we are operating from a higher calling. It is here that we are our best selves, able to make the greatest contribution to society. When you are in this state you are the most powerful, and you feel the most content. Worries seem to just melt away. You are the fish that swims because that's what fish do. You are the eagle that soars because it is hardwired in your nature. You are using your natural gifts. Your are authentic, uniquely you. Welcome to the world of Pull Now.

TOSS THE CARROTS AND THE STICKS

Our culture is mostly based on the premise that if you do this you get that—rewards. And if you don't do this you get that—punishment. We are told that everything boils down to avoiding pain or gaining pleasure. While there is no debating the short-term utility of these basic tenets of behavioral science, they are woefully inadequate to fulfilling and optimizing human potential. The premise that we are all horses in a herd longing for carrots and afraid of sticks is a paradigm that destroys passion, creativity and happiness in our work and personal lives. It denies us our best life and a far more satisfying career. It keeps people uninspired and de-motivated. We become eagles in cages and dolphins in small tanks.

Case in point: I have been a part of an industry (financial services) that really likes carrots—big carrots. And as far as the sticks go, well, let's just say that not getting a carrot proved an effective stick. (By the way, while I will continue to call upon examples from the world of financial services to illustrate some of the points we will explore from time to time, I trust that, no matter what kind of work you do, you will recognize the basic idea and, where needed, translate it into your own professional sphere.)

The vast majority of individuals who come into the financial services industry are what we would traditionally call "money-motivated." I was drawn to this industry as a young man for the same reasons as many others—an opportunity to work in an exciting, fast-paced business where I could get paid for results, not just tenure or office politics. The failure rate of brokers is staggering. I'd venture to say that less than one percent of those in my original training class are still working as advisors today. Those who made it always seem to quote that fallout rate fondly. It's kind of like the Marine Corps—the few, the proud, the surviving brokers. We were the ones who could take what the industry and the environment dished out. But the good news was always, well, at least the pay is decent. In a business of making money for others, making money for yourself goes with the territory. I remember, after having a record month in sales, being taken out to my first fancy steakhouse, complete with expensive tablecloths and doting waiters. I can still see the wine menu, the crystal glasses, the sizzling hunk of red meat overflowing with juices as the cabernet flowed along with congratulatory toasts from my boss.

The idea of pursuing a career focused on money had cast an early spell on me as I grew up with middle-class parents who were self-described workaholics. My dad worked several jobs to provide for our family and my mom was one of the original "super moms," juggling a household and a full-time teaching career. I was determined to select and focus on a single career that I believed would provide very well for my own family one day. As it happened, I was highly successful in this endeavor. I was earning a six-figure income by the age of 24 and always considered myself as someone fitting the classic mold within the industry. When I was a branch manager, this was one of the qualities I would attempt to measure in the hiring process. The more money-motivated the better. If a job candidate had never made much money, that was usually a sign that money was not important enough to them—particularly if they were over 40.

But recently, as I watched this industry go through major upheaval, I felt compelled to indulge in some Jerry McGuire-type confessional ranting. When I looked at what was happening in the industry within the context of my in-depth experience as a financial advisor, branch manager, home office executive and advisor trainer and coach, it was gut wrenching. The carnage among investors and advisors has been staggering. As you read this list, see if you can think about a more de-motivating environment for both:

Many client portfolios down by half, some even more.
The media reminding people every day just how bad it is.

Advisors were engulfed in toxic shame about the performance of portfolios and worried about their own survival in the industry.

If you think it's tough being an investor, try being an advisor when everyone thinks you are a bottom feeder. So how does this play into Pull? It's simply that when the primary motivator within an industry (namely how much money you can make for yourself) is wiped out, we are forced to ask, "What's left?" If I'm an advisor and I've been pro-grammed all my career to tie my own self-esteem to my own personal production, I've just had the rug pulled out from under me. When I've been measured against my peers based on the amount of revenue I pro-duce, I wonder whether that was ever really a good measure at all. As an advisor, am I really no better than a blackjack dealer in Vegas? Sure, I try to make playing the game as enjoyable as possible, but I never consid-ered what I did for a living as entertainment. I played an important role in allocating capital. But the reality was that as the economy tanked the folks who sat at my table got poorer, which produces massive amounts of guilt and shame. To come back to that phrase that Warren Buffet once used regarding tough times:

> "It's only when the tide goes out that you learn who's been swimming naked."

During the breakdown of my industry we might as well have stuck up a sign that reads, "Caution, you are entering a nude beach." We were exposed. But as time has gone on, many of us who swam in the financial services industry have been learning lessons that might provide all of us a new pair of swim trunks.

LIVING BY THE PUSH

Let me paint a picture of how it used to be in our industry. My branch manager used to keep a candy jar loaded with goodies next to a notebook outside his office that was updated daily to show what everybody did that previous day in commissions. And it showed how much each consultant had in assets under management. I confess, I was addicted to looking at that book. As a competitive person, I was constantly measuring my performance relative to others in my office. And the manager was smart enough to feed this every chance he got. He would send out recognition memos that rewarded performers and shamed non-performers. And he walked around the branch like a plantation owner monitoring the work of his slaves. Don't get me wrong, he was simply doing the best he could with what he thought he needed to do to be successful. But what was the price?

Whenever a broker left or was fired, all their accounts were distributed among the survivors. As it turned out, this was a very politically driven process and was used by the manager as a way to reward and punish. It was common practice in those days for a manager to decide to "make" someone much more successful through inherited accounts. In fact, it was the fastest way to the top. But it bred a branch culture that made us suspicious and often hostile to each other. Sometimes it felt like I was a member of the pioneering Donner party and the guy riding on the horse next to mine might be my next meal. It's true in sales that you eat what you kill, but does that have to include your colleagues?

Like an abusive behavior passed down to the next generation, I carried many of these "motivational tools" with me in my management career. I recall putting out a candy jar and placing the daily production run beside it. I would pass out recognition memos. I would leave newer advisors in cubicles and dangle glassed-in offices as carrots. Occasionally, a failing trainee would have to be fired and I would use that potential punishment as a means to motivate other trainees. I was using "the push."

One day I was surprised when one of my newer financial consultants piped up and protested some of my methods. She explained to me that making the daily production run so visible was a de-motivator. Initially, I dismissed her feedback as just not being able to compete with the rest of the pack. Only many years later did I come to realize that some of these traditional methods of motivation not only didn't work at the time, they probably had the opposite impact.

INSTEAD OF PUSH, FIND THE PULL:
6 QUESTIONS TO UNLOCK YOUR INTRINSIC DRIVE VAULT

If you want to maximize your potential, use tough times as a reason to explore what really makes you tick. Instead of looking for extrinsic drivers (the push) find your intrinsic drivers (the pull). How do you go about finding your Pull? Here are some questions to guide you.

1. Where are the important clues from your childhood?

If you want to identify ways to define what really pulls you, it will help to comb through your past. Use these questions about childhood to get you started.

- When nobody was looking and there were no external rewards or punishments, what activities brought you the most joy and satisfaction?

- When you look back, what things do you remember doing that seemed to come easy to you but were relatively difficult for others your age?

- Who were the people in your life that you most admired growing up? Why did you admire them? What did they do as a vocation? What skills or accomplishments did you admire?

- What positive experiences stand out most in your mind from your childhood?

- When you were with others your own age, what role did you play?

- How would somebody who knew you describe you?

- What were your favorite and least favorite subjects in school?

- When you think about times when you were most engaged in an activity or a subject, do you see recurring patterns or themes that stand out?

Often the apple doesn't fall far from the tree. When I would watch *The Wizard of Oz* I was always fascinated with how the story ends. As it turns out, Dorothy had the power all along to get home—she just didn't realize that the solution was literally right under her nose. Sometimes genetics can be like that. I think everyone initially resists the idea that somehow they are like their parents because it's human nature to want to be unique, to make our own choices and create our own destiny. It's also true that many kids don't grow up with role model parents and spend a lifetime distancing themselves from their parents' control or influence.

In many respects, this is the purpose of adolescence. We can see the importance of this separation whenever we revisit our family of origin at a holiday such as Thanksgiving, when we tend to revert back to old roles in the family dynamic. Once our parents reach a certain age, there may even be a sort of role reversal, with the kids taking on the role of the parent with reprimands and lectures reminiscent of the teenage years. But if we are able to gain perspective as we age, we can benefit immensely from accepting the parts of ourselves that may be hardwired at birth.

This really hit home with me after the birth of my son. So many things about him remind me of myself, it's like looking in the mirror. And while that isn't always comfortable, it's a learning opportunity. I've grown to accept and even greatly appreciate some of the pull that I've inherited. And what is fascinating is that the more research I do into my family tree, the more pull I have in common with my ancestors. For example, it turns out I come from a long line of preachers and teachers. No wonder I like to speak to groups of people!

I grew up watching my dad in the pulpit most Sundays and, as much as I used to cringe at the thought, I am a preacher's kid. Some of my fondest memories come from my mother playing the piano and watching her write original scores of music for her school productions. One of the things I relish about being a speaker is creating my own "shows." In her early years, she played the church piano while Dad preached. There were many Saturday nights when I would go into his study and listen to him preparing for the Sunday service. He was also a college professor with enormous intellect, warmth and natural teaching ability, but I tended to see him "in action" more in his preacher role. To this day, my 84-year-old dad is invited to speak in the pulpit on occasion. And my mother, also 84, delights groups with her beautiful piano playing.

What good qualities did you inherit from your folks? It's likely that there are many wonderful gifts—many interests, talents and strengths that combine to form your Pull. They're just waiting for you to discover and enjoy them if you will but look under your nose.

2. Are you "a natural" at something?

Our culture gives mixed messages when it comes to talent and ability. On one hand, we applaud it and encourage it. But on the other hand we are often shy when it comes to embracing it or valuing it. This cautious tone might come from our puritanical roots. If we don't have to work at something, then by definition it must not have a high value. This is nonsense. We are all "naturals" at something. And this is something we should not only be proud of, we should leverage it to the utmost degree.

These are gifts. And with those gifts come a responsibility to use them in some positive way.

It's highly likely that the biggest contributions you will make in your lifetime will come from something where you had some raw talent. Now, I'm not discounting hard work—quite the contrary. When you are working in a field or an area where you have natural raw gifts, you can contribute far more than in areas where you have fewer raw gifts. What would you do even if you weren't paid to do it? What activities or subject matters can get you so engrossed in that you lose all track of time? Have you ever done something that caused someone to label you "a natural?"

3. What stirs your curiosity?

One of the hallmarks of childhood that we tend to lose as adults is our curiosity. If you ever find yourself bored with what you are doing, the best anecdote is a dose of curiosity. In fact, when you are curious it's impossible to be bored. When you enter a bookstore, notice which section you find yourself browsing through. If you did an inventory of all the books you've ever purchased, what would be some of the common themes? When you are flipping channels at home, what do you find most entertaining or educational? Have you ever attended a workshop, seminar or lecture that was not part of a formal education curriculum? What were the subjects? If you were to host a dinner party, which three people whom you have never met would you invite if you knew for sure they would accept? If you could travel to one destination on earth where you have never been, where would you go and why? If you could master another language, which would it be and why? If you had a time machine and could travel back in time to any period of the earth's history, when would it be? Where would it be? Imagine that you could discover one major breakthrough in the field of your choice, what would it be?

4. What can you see that others don't?

Have you ever been with a group of people trying to solve a problem and the solution was obvious to you but not to the others? Have you ever felt like you were in a horror movie and everyone else around you can't see the bad guy coming but you can? The amount of clarity, certainty and confidence you have when presented with a particular challenge can give you clues about where you should focus your attention. If you are in a forest where others are lost but you seem to be blazing new trails, you are probably barking up the right tree. Pay attention to your track record when evaluating your skill levels. Did you see it coming, but for whatever reason fail to act? What would have happened had you paid attention to your gut? Is there an area where you seem to be as good or better than the so-called experts?

5. What really energizes you?

When you strike oil, the image of a well gushing with the black stuff shooting out everywhere comes to mind. It flows effortlessly and there is a sense that there are huge reserves under the surface. The flow can go on and on. So it is when you have identified a pull. It's like you struck it rich and are totally energized by it.

Have you ever done a task where it felt like your energy level actually increased during the process of completing the task? This is what happens when you are performing in an area energizing to you. If you could do one type of activity all day long in your work, what would it be? If you were gauging the level of "psychic income" derived from a particular activity, where would you find the biggest payoffs? Are there areas where you seem to complete tasks with much greater speed than others? Do you ever feel like you are in a movie and everyone else is moving in slow motion? Pay attention to that spark, that current that revs up your batteries. You'll need that extra juice when times are tough.

6. What gives you pure joy?

Finally, when it comes to discovering your Pull, listen to your heart. Have you ever done something in your capacity at work that filled you with unbridled joy? Have you found happiness in a certain pursuit more than any other? When you are alone and ask yourself, "Am I happy doing what I'm doing?" what answer do you get back? Which work activities give you the most pleasure? Think back to the last time you smiled really big at work—what were you doing? Can you find a common theme or pattern that gives you clues of what type of work might give you the most joy? Going back to some of our cultural hang-ups, at some point somebody decided that anything worth doing at work was not going to be fun. Nothing could be further from the truth. It's not that everything you do in any job or profession will cause you to wear a permanent grin on your face. It's just that when you find your Pull, you will have far more moments of pure joy.

I remember moderating an event of the top 100 financial advisors—it's called the Barrons 100. The number-one advisor gave a talk on what he thought was the key to his success. Many were surprised to hear that his major goal when he gets up every morning is to find a way to have fun with his work that day. We tend to discount the importance of having fun in our everyday work life. We need to look for the fun. And if we look hard enough we will find it. But it is far easier to find that fun after you've found your Pull.

Whether you call these strengths, gifts, talents, abilities, hardwiring or whatever, the fact is that it is a moral imperative that you identify these resources in your life.

HOW TO USE YOUR PULL

If you study the lives of people with great influence, the one common thread you will find is that at some critical point in their lives, when the heat was on, their pull became more than just a silent inner voice. It evolved into a compelling mission of meaning and purpose. Simply put, we can either use our pull or lose our pull. And if your pull is idling like a vintage car on blocks in a garage or a set of paintbrushes in a closet, it's time to actually use your pull.

Once you have identified your Pull then the next step is to:

Clarify your values

When you are trying to decide how to use your Pull, it's critical to first know your boundaries. Our boundaries define us and frame our lives, giving us the proper context to make choices that will be in harmony with what is most important. As Steven Covey says, as you are climbing the ladder of success, make sure you have it leaning up against the right wall. Here are some questions to help you clarify what's most important.

- What qualities of character do you most admire in others (integrity, hard working, loyalty, etc.)?

- How do you define success (family, career, relationships, etc.)?

- What emotional states do you value most (joy, contentment, humor, gratitude, peace of mind, etc.)?

- How would you want someone who knows you best to describe you to someone whom you've never met?

Allow yourself to dream

In my business coaching, it's amazing how quickly dreams get shot down. And it's not me or other people doing the shooting, it's the individual getting coached! Many of us are afraid to articulate what we really want. It might be fear of failure, or it might even be a fear of success (you'll be surprised how many people subconsciously sabotage success because of personal issues from childhood). It's absolutely necessary to open your mind and your imagination and let yourself dream.

Pretend that you have found a magic lantern and a genie pops out and actually gives you three wishes. What would they be? What have you always wanted to do but were afraid to try? What would you dare to do if you were certain of success? How would you spend your time if you had all the resources you needed? What would you do if you found out you only had three years to live? What have you always said you would like to accomplish but have been putting off for "better timing?" Before you start shooting down all those idea balloons, at least let them get airborne. You might be amazed at how far they fly.

Define purpose

Once you have established the parameters of what is most important to you, it's now time to define your purpose. This can be through the development of a personal mission statement or a more narrowly defined set of objectives. It should be something that makes a statement about how you live your values, the "why" behind how you intend to use your Pull. Here is my personal mission statement again to help get you writing your own:

"My mission is to inspire, entertain, educate, coach and advise people in ways that maximize their potential and performance—to lead them on a journey of personal and professional development, purposeful contribution, financial success and lifelong goal achievement. And to have more fun and laughs along the way."

Your purpose will serve as a reference, a beacon and a guide on your journey. When you know your purpose, it provides meaning to everything you do. If you question something you are about to do, refer back to your purpose and ask yourself if this is something that is in alignment with your purpose or something that detracts from your purpose.

Create a compelling vision

When you have defined and articulated your purpose, it's time to let your imagination paint the picture of a compelling vision. Throughout the ages, there have been great leaders who have changed the world. And it all started with a compelling vision. If your values and your purpose are the screenplay, your vision is the actual movie. And you should make this a major motion picture, using the theater of your mind. Imagine yourself walking along the sand or on your favorite trail reflecting on all the things you are grateful for in your life. Create vivid images of those things as if they are already happening right now. The brighter the colors the better, and the more animated the action the better. How are these pictures making you feel?

Let yourself experience all the emotions that come with each frame of the movie. Describe all the benefits that will come with this vision. Focus on the contributions you are now able to make because of what you've been able to achieve. Imagine walking into a room, surrounded by feelings of love and warmth, and suddenly everyone you know is there and they all spontaneously jump to their feet with applause. You then greet each one of them and they describe to you what a difference you have made in their lives and how without you all these wonderful things would not have been possible.

Set meaningful goals with deadlines

Now it's time to put together an action plan to accelerate your progress towards your goals. I once read that a vision without goals is a wish. Goals allow you to focus your energy to make your compelling vision a reality. Earl Nightingale said, "Happiness is the progressive realization of a worthy goal or ideal." This means that having goals is not just a one-time exercise. It's a habit that gets far less attention and respect than it should in our school system and in organizations in general. Like mile markers along the highway of your journey, goals give you markers so you can measure your progress. It's also important to write your goals down. The very act of writing (or typing) helps program your goals into your subconscious and propel you toward your destination. Your goals should be as specific as possible. Vagueness leads to distraction along your path. Have you noticed there is just something about somebody who knows where they are going?

Your new career or business path

Now that you have identified your Pull, clarified your values, created a compelling vision and set your new goals, it's likely that you might be strongly considering a new career or business path. Here are some questions and tips as you go through the thought process.

- What are you currently doing that you would like to keep doing?

- What are you currently doing that you want to stop doing?

- If you decide to stay where you are, is there a way to delegate those tasks that drain you the most? Is there a way to partner with someone whereby you take on a task they don't like and they take on a task you don't like?

- Who do you know who is already doing what you would like to be doing? Take the time to interview those who are getting the results you want. Ask for their advice. You will find most people willing to help if you approach them correctly.

- If you are not willing to leave what you are doing because of financial or other reasons, is there a way to embark on a new path in your spare time?

- Will a new path require that you go back to school to receive another degree?

- How will your new career or business path impact your family?

- Take an inventory of all your work experience and look for patterns of success and failure.

- Using the 80–20 rule, it's highly likely that 20 percent of your skill set is responsible for 80 percent of your success. Make sure you identify and appreciate that 20 percent.

- At the same time, there may be weaknesses that keep showing up as a pattern. Instead of wasting too much time fretting over those, use a new path as a means to jettison that baggage.

- Do you prefer to work individually or as part of a team?

- Are you more extroverted or introverted?

- Are you detail-oriented or do you prefer big-picture thinking?

- Do you like working with your hands or more with your brain?

- Are you more analytical in your thinking or more creative?

- Do you prefer to be moving around a lot at work or are you fine sitting at a desk?

- Do you prefer to be a star performer or more of a role player?

- How do you feel about travel in your job or business?

- Do you have the capital to launch your own business?

- Have you considered bringing on a partner of partners?

When 2 + 2 = 5

If part of your new career or business path involves joining or leading a team, there are many "best practices" you should keep in mind in the process. In my coaching work with financial advisor teams, one of the first things we do is an assessment of who is currently doing what. Then we ask each team member to rank their level of skill at doing each task and their corresponding level of enjoyment. We also administer some type of personality test to determine preferences, relative strengths and weaknesses. With this information we can begin to have a conversation around creating synergy on a team where 2 + 2 can indeed equal 5.

When you see problems emerge on teams and the boat seems to be careening down the rapids towards a steep waterfall, you can usually look back and see signs of trouble beginning upstream. The rudder was set in the wrong direction originally and the wrong crew members were inefficiently scrambling, and it just took a while before it became obvious to everyone. If you are the one in charge of forming a team, here are some tips to help you resource and hire the right candidates.

Look in your own backyard first. Before you spend a lot of time, money and effort looking for talent outside your world, make sure you look in your own backyard first. There is a syndrome I've observed over the years that goes something like this: "The best recruits are always from out of town." We tend to discount people and things that are the most familiar. For example, in my hometown of Athens, Georgia, a high school player was less highly regarded by the University of Georgia recruiting staff than a player of similar talent from a different zip code. The conventional wisdom was that many of them would just "walk on" to be a Bulldog, so there was no need to waste scholarship dollars on those players willing to play for "free."

If you are making a move within your own company, is there somebody with whom you've done a project who you know would make a superb full-time partner or team member? If you are launching your own business, are there people you already know who used to work for you or your company with whom you've had prior experience? Are there neighbors or members of your church who might make good business partners? Have you always wanted to start a family business? If you have older kids looking for work, maybe this is the perfect time to move forward with that venture. The bottom line is make sure you take time to get to know the local talent first; you might just find a diamond.

Think opposite. Many people consider forming a team with people because they are already friends. While it's important to like the person, this approach is fraught with danger. If the other partner is too similar, they will not bring the complementary skill sets to the table that you will need to be successful. For example, in the world of financial advisors, we often see partners who may be good at getting new clients but lousy at servicing existing clients. It's far better to have someone focused on getting outside the office to cultivate new client relationships and someone inside doing the research, financial planning, administration, etc. It's very difficult to effectively wear all the hats. If you are good at the details, look for others who might be better at the big picture. If you are a great talker, find someone who is a great listener. If you are disorganized, find someone who is meticulous. If you are good with numbers, find someone who is good with words. If you are good with computers, find someone who is good over the phone. Obviously it may be necessary to find someone with multiple skills. The point is not to be attracted to someone just because they are like you. It's the opposite that might be the better answer.

Beware the Jack of all trades, expert at none. When you are considering the complementary skill sets of others, think of yourself as a coach trying to field a winning team. If this were a football team, you would need to know the strength, speed and agility of each player so you could assign the proper role and execute a winning game plan. It's the same when evaluating team players in business. It's better to look at each prospect in the context of what role you want them to play. If you find someone who seems to do it all, make sure you examine that assumption closely. Often it's the jack of all trades that turns out to be the expert of none. What you want to assemble is a team of experts— role players to help you reach your business or career goals.

If you determine that a change is in order, consider teaming with others who have complementary pull and you will find $2 + 2 = 5$.

5

Bob as Bill: Lessons from a Bill Clinton Impersonator

Are you an entrepreneur, always keeping an eye out for a new venture, new direction, or totally new idea? Are you following a business career with a multifaceted resume that includes a skill or two that may prompt an initial double-take from a prospective employer? Most of us have performed jobs or tasks that might be considered "a little bit different." Nothing wrong with that. In fact, I believe that part of living *The Undaunted Life* is to be aware of, and value, what we may be able to do that few others can. I had one of those experiences several years ago. It's a skill, you might say, that I still "carry" with me. I'm going to tell you the story of what it is, how it came to be, and what I learned from the experience that any of us can apply to business and life.

Back in 1992 a relatively unknown former governor of Arkansas came onto the national stage. One night I got a phone call from my folks. "You've got to see this guy running for president," they said. "Oh my god, he looks just like you!" Over the next several days other family and friends called to tell me the same thing. When I saw him on TV the first time, I nearly fell out of my chair. I have to admit it was a bit weird at first, especially when they showed him in his younger years as governor. And what was more bizarre was that the more I learned about this candidate, the more I realized we had much in common. For starters, we are the same height and both have fair skin. Our facial features and body frame are quite similar. We both grew up in the south with the corresponding Southern drawl. We both played the saxophone in high school. And to top it off, I've always been a bit of a political junkie.

Yes, there was no doubt; I had an uncanny resemblance to this presidential hopeful. But I had a burgeoning career as a branch manager at Merrill Lynch, the largest brokerage firm in the country. So at first I didn't seriously consider taking advantage of my look-a-like status. Then one day I was joking around with a buddy who was egging me on to do something about my "dead ringer" status and I suddenly blurted out, "I bet you I can get on *The Tonight Show* with Jay Leno!" I'm not sure where that wild notion came from, but this declaration turned out to be the beginning of Bob as Bill. And it set the wheels in motion for quite an adventure in my life in the months and years ahead, an adventure that I now use to teach business lessons to my coaching clients.

7 BUSINESS LESSONS I LEARNED AS BILL CLINTON

Lesson #1—Be Authentic: How to leverage the one thing that can't be copied, downsized, outsourced or commoditized

It soon became my personal mission to deliver on what I declared to my friend. It started with some research. I quickly ascertained that I needed to gray my hair and get some photos taken. Not just any photographer was going to do, so I discovered a guy in Hollywood that specialized in photos for celebrity look-a-likes. I drove to his studio on a Saturday morning and he quickly got excited about the possibilities. I was a sponge, asking questions about this whole look-a-like business. I did not share with him my *Tonight Show* goal, only that I wanted to get some photos out there to test the waters. We settled in on a single page with two shots: one with me looking up in almost a southern preacher pose with my hands clasped in prayer, hoping for a winning election day. The other photo had me holding a tenor saxophone with dark sunglasses to resemble Bill Clinton's appearance on *The Arsenio Hall Show*.

Since I was a veteran at cold-calling, I thought nothing of simply picking up the phone and trying to get Jay Leno on the phone. Of course, I was not able to get through but did manage to reach his secretary. And somehow I convinced her she that she could be the one credited with discovering the next great act on *The Tonight Show*. I figured since Jay was new on the show, they might be open to something that was hot in the news right now. I sent the photos by FedEx and got a call back the next day. She informed me that "the writers are interested in meeting you."

After some haggling with the gatekeeper at the NBC Studios parking lot, he finally found the right contact person on *The Tonight Show* staff to grant me a parking pass. I was then greeted at a door and escorted to the heart of *The Tonight Show* studio, passing through a maze of security checkpoints and studios for other network shows. As I walked by people, I watched their shock turned to a smile—a good sign! We finally reached a long stairwell and the last checkpoint where I was asked to open the case I was holding. You see, I had come fully armed and prepared—I brought a tenor saxophone like the one Clinton liked to play. I figured that could be the one thing that separated me from other competitors.

I was brought into a room full of idea white boards, photos and graphic designer work tables. After a few minutes a team of writers walked in and I was thoroughly interviewed. They asked me everything from where I was from, to what I did for a living, where was I living now, my associations. Then they all seemed to look at each other with nods and confirming glances as the leader simply said, "Well, I guess it's time you met Jay." A few minutes later, Jay Leno walked in the room wearing blue jeans and a matching casual blue button-down collar shirt. I have to tell you, this guy is one of the most genuine people you could ever meet. What you see on TV is the way he is in real life. He started wisecracking the moment he walked in the door and started looking me over. He asked if my hair was real, and I explained it was sprayed and my real color was red. He asked whether I was associated with an agency. It was at this moment that I knew this answer might blow it for me, but I told him I was doing this on my own and was not affiliated with any agency. He responded with that trademark Jay Leno grin and said, "Good, that means we don't have to deal with that ____."

There were many memorable moments for me on the show, and

some that were forgettable (like the time I had to be chased by the Oscar Mayer Wienermobile truck through Johnny Carson Park. Clinton loved burgers and the hot dog lobby was getting pretty upset about all the attention they were getting). But I have to say my favorite performance was called *Victoria's Secret Service.*

We see an up-close shot of the presidential seal, with drums rolling in the background. The announcer says, "He's young, he's handsome, he's the President of the United States. And when it comes to protecting him, ordinary Secret Service Agents just won't do." (The camera pans back to reveal me behind the podium surrounded by three beautiful ladies in lingerie wearing sunglasses and carrying themselves like agents.) The voice then says, "He needs Victoria's Secret Service . . . highly trained, thoroughly professional . . . drop-dead gorgeous. Victoria's Secret Service. Lookin' out . . . lookin' good. Coming to NBC."

As you can imagine, this breakthrough sent me on a high, a bit like being elected president! Of course, it wasn't always rosy being Bob as Bill. When people would ask what it was like looking like the most powerful man in the world, I would answer that it was a roller coaster ride. When Bill Clinton was first running for office and first elected president, it was an exhilarating experience to walk out on stage and seemingly be admired for somebody I wasn't. But a funny thing happened when the scandals started to hit—it wasn't nearly as much fun. In fact, there were people I met who actually hated Clinton so badly, guess what? They started to hate me too!

But here's part of what I learned that can be helpful to you: know who you are and how to appropriately utilize it. If you are going through tough times, recognize that the first thing you need to do is look inward and get to know exactly who you are. That means discovering your authentic self. In a world where everything is constantly changing, your best defense is simply staying true to yourself in all situations. That's being able to look yourself in the mirror and feel good about what you see and the person you are becoming. Those who are able to project their authenticity to others are at a distinct advantage in the marketplace. Imagine an authenticity meter and the higher your reading, the more control you have over your destiny, the more power you have to influence others and the happier you'll be in whatever you choose to do in life. Here are some specific strategies to boost your authenticity meter.

Ask yourself what you can do that is not easily replicated. The emergence of China as an economic superpower and adversary has been partly due to the trend to design things here in the U.S. but build them there. Critics point out that we have lost our manufacturing base and it's only a matter of time before the Chinese "reverse engineer" our products and ultimately take the lead in innovation and design. We can all learn lessons from history on this subject. Remember when "made in Japan" was a joke? Then along came Honda, Lexus and Sony to dominate their respective categories. Imitation may be the best form of flattery but it can also lead to the unemployment line if your job, product or even business can be easily and cheaply copied or duplicated. If you viewed yourself as your own personal services corporation, how easy would it be to replicate what you do? Ask yourself what is unique about what you do compared to the alternatives in the marketplace. Believe me, even if you are not asking the questions, your boss and others in your organization are—it's their job. Remember the ad from Coca-Cola: "There ain't nothing like the real thing baby, nothing like the real thing?" Make sure what you do is the "real thing," not a cheap imitation.

Become downsize-proof. There is a lot of jargon in the business world to describe being fired. One of my favorites is "downsized." It implies that you were too big in the first place and now you just don't fit anymore. In tough times, every business leader has either already downsized, is going to downsize or is considering a downsize. It's a business reality. So the question is how can you make yourself "downsize-proof?" The first thing is to do a realistic assessment of why you are on the payroll. Are you considered someone who is bringing in the revenue or are you in some kind of supporting role? The closer you are to the revenue side of any business the better your job security. The last thing a company wants to do is cut off their revenue sources in tough times. Do you know exactly how much revenue can be attributed to your efforts? If you are not in a commission sales situation where you eat what you kill, make sure you align yourself with projects that are viewed as revenue enhancing and must-have as opposed to projects where there is limited return on investment visibility.

Be "outsource" proof. In Thomas Friedman's book, *The World Is Flat,* he makes a strong case that outsourcing is a permanent trend that is just getting started. Technology is enabling collaboration and work sharing on a scale most of us could not even imagine a few years ago. When a qualified medical doctor in India can examine a set of x-rays from a patient in the U.S. over the worldwide web at a dramatically lower cost, we've clearly entered a new dimension in outsourcing. It's one thing to have a call center answering basic questions about a credit card charge, but it's another thing to have high-value, complex problems being worked on and solved with a click of a mouse over great distances. We will soon see this tsunami hit the shores of every major industry. Imagine having your tax return handled or an engineering design work done on line by a highly qualified person at a fraction of the cost, maybe even in a fraction of the time. It's the sheer speed of what can be cranked out that is staggering in this new age.

Given this shift, it's time to at least get yourself "outsource resistant" or ideally "outsource proof." It's like picking a pair of shoes to wear on a muddy hike in the rain. You already know those flimsy tennis shoes you've been wearing won't cut it on this terrain. It's just a matter of choosing between shoes lined with vinyl or Gore-tex. Both will keep the water out, but it's the Gore-tex that allows your feet to breathe easier. Here are some tips to protect yourself when you see the outsource wave on your weather radar.

- Invest in stocks of companies that will benefit from outsourcing as a hedge against your own job loss.

- Consider pursuing a career or starting a business in a service area where technology impact is minimal. Areas such as plumbing or electrical contracting require hands-on expertise, applying physical on-site skill.

- Surf the wave. If you can't fight the wave, maybe you should try to surf it. Spot long-term trends and position yourself to take advantage of it. Consider the aging population. There will be growing demand for elder care and medical services. Consider educational services that cater to those seeking to change careers.

- Take a look around your shop and see what other jobs you can do to boost your value. Many employers are already trying to get one person to do the job of two. It's far better to be proactive and initiate such a proposal than to wait until your boss suggests it.

- Be prepared to reinvent your own job responsibilities, which may include the idea that you can also do the job of someone reporting to you now. I know that sounds Machiavellian, but this scenario is playing out all over the place and you should have a contingency plan with this in mind.

Determine if you are a commodity. If you watch the price of oil, gold or pork bellies you will see that the value of any commodity is extremely volatile and unpredictable. Are you in a job or position that is so tied to the economy that you are always in constant fear of a downturn? There are very few recession-proof businesses. We've all heard how Hershey kept the town by the same name alive and well in the Great Depression. Chocolate, it seems, is in demand no matter what the size of the paycheck or even if there isn't one. My grandparents lived in Houston and it's always been sort of a boom/bust town, mainly because its fate is so closely tied to oil. We all know what happened to Enron, but the point is we should not be naive about the cyclical nature of some industries and businesses. If you are in a business closely tied to the business cycle, it's important to sock even more nuts away for the inevitable winter. But we can all become commoditized if we are not watchful and keep our skills on the cutting edge.

I remember as a branch manager having a wire operator get excited when she learned we were going to automate almost all of the order entry functions so that advisors could enter orders on their own without her assistance. She thought her job was going to suddenly get easier, which it indeed did. The point she missed was that her job just saw a huge drop in value. She was still able to provide some cashiering functions, but when the markets got soft and I had to trim fixed costs in the branch, guess what happened? That's right, we had to let her go.

Make sure who you are and what you offer are the real deal. When times are tough, it's easy to tell the difference between dead weight and gold.

Lesson #2—Empathy power: How to listen and understand your way to the top

When I was perfecting my Bill Clinton impersonation, I watched tapes of the presidential debates over and over to pick up on mannerisms, gestures and speech patterns. And one of the things that became clear in that campaign was that Bill Clinton had mastered a very powerful skill. He was able to identify with what the average American was going through at that time. He told us, "I can feel your pain." What he was using was the power of empathy. And there is none better at it than Bill Clinton. I've never had the pleasure of meeting him in person, but those who have claim that he pulls you in with incredible magnetic force. It's said that he can make a person feel that they are the only person in the world at that moment. We all got a front-row seat to watch a master show us how to listen and understand your way to the top, at least until the Monica Lewinsky scandal left us feeling Clinton's pain.

One could argue that when it comes to people skills, listening with a caring and understanding ear is the fastest way to connect with people at all levels. Yet the key to effective empathy is for the other person to feel you have all the time in the world to listen. It's like a fine wine, the taste gets better with age, or the more the conversation seems to linger on each caring word or gesture. Here are some suggestions I learned from the master himself about how to ramp up your Empathy Power.

Body language is critical. Remember how Bill Clinton always seemed to be nodding yes. This is saying, "I hear you, you are important, I understand where you are coming from."

Pause before replying. Whenever you see Bill Clinton on *Larry King Live*, it's fascinating just how patient he is when a caller is asking a question. Here's a former president who was the most powerful man in the world, yet he humbles himself to hear someone out about a range of issues. He never interrupts or rushes the conversation. When you pause before replying, you are communicating great respect to the other person.

Smile to show acceptance and approval. It's so basic and fundamental that we have a tendency to forget how powerful a simple smile can be in human relations. No matter where you are from, no matter what language you speak, no matter your social status or economic standing, it's a smile that is universally understood as a signal that the other person is accepted and liked. A smile may be the fastest way to start winning others over. Why? Because we all have a deep need to be liked and, when we smile at another human being, we are saying in a non-verbal unequivocal way, "I like you." If you are self-conscious about your teeth or your smile, it is worth the investment to see a dentist and explore all the ways to brighten your smile. The better you feel about your smile, the more likely you are to smile. The more you smile the better you feel about yourself and the world around you. Even when you are talking on the phone, "smile into the phone." We form a mental image and it's always more pleasant to have a conversation with someone who likes what we are saying.

Practice active listening. During the presidential debates, there was a new format introduced that has now become a standard form—the town hall meeting. This format was tailor-made for Bill Clinton. You could see that whenever an audience member asked a question, Clinton would first thank the person for the question, then he would repeat the question for clarification. This would usually be followed by an "I can feel your pain"-type response, and finally the answer. If you engage in that degree of active listening in any business interaction, you will stand out.

Lesson #3—Be a "Comeback Kid" regardless of the economy or the competition

During a recent Oscar Awards, it was fascinating to see the actor Mickey Rourke being considered for Best Actor for his portrayal of an aging athlete in *The Wrestler*. This was his comeback role after being down in the dumps for many years from self-inflicted wounds. Though Rourke didn't win, it was his comeback that made all the headlines. As Americans, we love a comeback story. And when it comes to rebounding from self-inflicted wounds, few will ever rival Bill Clinton. During his time as president, Clinton took more than his share of punches but he just didn't give up.

Any of us can develop that kind of tenacity and resilience. When I had been a broker at Merrill Lynch for only under a year, a new trainee was hired in the branch. He sat in the cubicle next to mine. He was old enough to be my father, but he had that "silver fox" look that would assure clients they were dealing with an established, sophisticated veteran broker. As I was cold-calling executives and business owners from a directory and getting rejected, he was "warm-calling" his friends and contacts. As I got to know him, I discovered he had been a highly paid sales manager. Since I knew Merrill didn't pay much to trainees, even with his background, I asked him why he was willing to take such a pay cut at this stage of his life. His answer both surprised and impressed me. First, he explained that he was bored with his old job. Then he said something I'll never forget, "I've always believed that real confidence was having the guts to start over."

Lesson #4—Flexibility as a virtue: How to "change" your way to success

After my appearance on *The Tonight Show*, I received many calls about doing gigs ranging from a convention in Tokyo to private Hollywood parties. Eventually, as Clinton left office and much of the spotlight shifted to other political figures (including his wife!), the calls tapered off. In the past few years, however, I've found myself brushing up on my act and taking Bob as Bill back on the road again. I even have a website now dedicated to my impersonator services at www.bobasbill. com. During my own personal discovery journey, I was reminded of the importance of having more fun and laughs, and part of that for me is doing this work. Besides, as I look back, I see so many valuable experiences in playing the role that I'm sure more insights are on the way. Here's one that will be hard to top.

One day a producer of *The Maury Povich Show* tracked me down and literally begged me to fly from Los Angeles to New York for a live taping of a show about women who fantasized about being with the president. They wanted me to be on the show because one of the girls had a dream about the president playing the saxophone for her. The problem was the call came in late Wednesday and the show was being taped early Friday morning. To make it I would have to fly out the next morning. The song they wanted me to play was Elvis Presley's "Heartbreak Hotel" (the same song Clinton had played on *The Arsenio Hall Show)*. After a long negotiation on the phone, I relented and agreed. She wanted me to be prepared to play the song on stage but we both agreed it would be better if we were able to get a "background tape" of the sound to accompany my live performance. I would then buy sheet music of the song to bring with me.

I practiced as best I could on short notice, but just before air time the producer threw me a curve ball: I was going to surprise everyone by popping out from behind the curtain at just the right moment playing "Heartbreak Hotel." The problem was that the scenario she described involved my parading around without my music to read. When I explained this to her, she asked a critical question. "Do you think you know the music well enough to play it without the music?" This was my moment of truth. I said, "I'll do it."

Positioned behind the curtain, I visualized what I needed to do and mimicked the key strokes on my sax in preparation. Then Maury said to the woman, "What would you do if Bill Clinton came on stage right now and played "Heartbreak Hotel?" Then the background tape started with a bass guitar riff that served as my queue. I had to hit that first note just right or the rest of the number just would not work. I stepped out and began playing. It certainly wasn't perfect but the audience began instinctively clapping along with the song until I was finished.

Here's the lesson: no matter how prepared we are we must maintain flexibility to change our approach based on circumstances. If we are too rigid, we miss opportunities. When that producer gave me that challenge, I knew that I needed to be flexible and stretch beyond my comfort zone so that I could take full advantage of the live performance opportunity. And you know what? I ended up improvising a whole series of movements across the stage as I played, just going with the flow. For most of us, it's during our moments of spontaneity that our best selves can come out. We are not only the most authentic at that point, we are usually the happiest. And that quality shines through.

Lesson #5—"Trust me": How to win people over and keep them on your side

Building trust is a tricky thing. Rebuilding it is even trickier once you've lost it. It's hard to imagine now but, after Pearl Harbor, were Japanese Americans were placed into prison camps because it was widely believed that the surprise attack meant that no Japanese could be trusted. Later the words "Made in Japan" meant don't trust the product to work. How ironic that not so many years later, we are driving Japanese-made cars and watching Japanese-made televisions because of their reputation for high quality.

Regardless of how you feel about Bill Clinton, one can't help but wonder what might have been had he not lost the trust of the American people. Ironically, it was another southern president that is most known for honesty and integrity—Jimmy Carter, from my home state of Georgia. Studying the Carter presidency highlights the difference between having trust in a leader and having confidence in a leader. I think when someone runs for president of the most powerful country in the world, it's the ultimate "trust me." Coming after the Watergate scandal and Nixon's resignation, Carter was a breath of fresh air. His integrity has always been apparent, but when he announced that there was a crisis of confidence, it had the unintended consequence of creating a lack of confidence in his leadership. Then the hostage crisis hit along with stag-flation and the rest is history.

The point is that it's impossible for us to reach our full potential if we don't first establish trust with the people in our world. This should not be a false choice between basic trust in your intentions (Carter) or trust in our raw ability to lead (Clinton). It should be a "twofer." The one should automatically come with the other.

When we see what happened on Wall Street and criminals like Bernie Madoff, it's a reminder that the biggest failures in life are indeed moral failures. Over time, honesty and integrity will separate you from the pack. One of the most basic questions we ask when we meet someone for the first time is, "Can I trust you?" Whenever you've lost trust, the most constructive thing you can do is to quickly get about the business of restoring that trust and your credibility. But how exactly can you do that? How can you win people over even after you've fallen short and keep them on your side? Here are some tips to help you build or rebuild a foundation of trust with your customers, clients, coworkers, family or friends in tough times.

Put yourself in their shoes. This goes back to empathy but takes it one step further. Remember as a kid learning how and when to say "I'm sorry"? Only when the apology was accepted could you move on. In business, it's important to go beyond the head nodding and actually take the time to apologize if need be, then get the facts about how this environment has directly impacted the situation. That means getting "belly to belly" with your clients or customers to discuss what happened and what it really means to them. In the financial advisor-client relationship, this means having an honest discussion of the results of specific recommendations and owning up to misjudgments that may have been made. If you are in sales or service it might be something related to a disruption or price increase at the wrong time. In your relationships, it might be an acknowledgment that you have not spent enough time together lately.

Do something to help. It's not enough to talk about it. Go into meetings prepared to offer something specific to help. Be proactive.

If you are the first to make concessions or reduce your price in a bad economic environment, you will go a long way toward building trust and loyalty. Another tactic is to offer to help a customer or client or business partner in ways that are unexpected. For example, if you want to have somebody loyal for life help them get their kid or grandkid a job. How about getting them new business? If you are someone referring people to them to build their business, it's almost certain to boost their trust and confidence in you.

Be consistent. There is nothing more toxic to trust than inconsistency. Many view this as simply lying. Have you been inconsistent in the past? Don't underestimate the shelf life of a little white lie or mixed messages. Successful people do what they say they are going to do. For example, do you always return phone calls within a short period of time? Do you have a habit of ignoring emails? Do you seem to always have a fresh excuse as to why you have not done what you said you would do? Are you constantly changing your story? Is there a disconnect between what you are saying and what your firm is saying? What about what your best clients are saying to others? We are seeing a phenomenon in the financial services industry called a "negative referral." What this means is that some clients are so unhappy they are actually warning their friends and family to stay away from firms or advisors. This kind of negative publicity can be quite damaging. I remember being told once that:

> It takes ten friends to compensate for one enemy.

Make contact with purpose. During bad times or good, the only way you can stay on top of what may be happening to others in your world is through regular contact. While technology such as email has made it easier to have some contact, it's important to make the contact meaningful and in person if possible. The most powerful tool in the presidential arsenal outside of nukes is the bully pulpit. It's the ability to reach out and contact the American people through direct communication.

How are you doing getting your message out? Do your customers or clients know what you are doing for them during uncertain times? Are you making your case to your boss, suppliers, coworkers? When it comes to your relationships, are you taking the time to let the people you care about know how much they mean to you? Maybe you can use challenging times to reconnect with old friends.

Lesson #6—Audacity: How to win big making bold moves in timid times
When the economy is down, the news is filled with stories about the need to scale back, to downsize, to expect less, to just hold on tight to what you have. This may very well be sound advice if taken in proper measure, but the reality is that most people succeed by making bold moves when everyone else around them is frozen and timid, shrinking away from life. Making bold moves isn't about striking out blindly, it's about being strategic and purposeful. It's about showing courage under fire. We have to tap our inner hero to swoop in and rescue ourselves and others in times of crisis.

> One of the secrets to success in life is to not be afraid to
> think big.

If you study highly successful people, you will see quantum leaps only after they allowed themselves to aim high. Don't expect somebody else to light that fire underneath you or whisper some magical words of encouragement. It's fear that holds most people back from fulfilling their potential. Audacity is the quality needed when the mood seems to favor caution. After all, if everyone else is taking a breather, it doesn't take as much effort to get out in front. Bill Clinton was the governor of a very small state. What made him think he could get all the way to the White House? When he shook hands with JFK, what went through his mind?

Ambition is a quality you must guard carefully if you want to advance in your career and in life. Those around you may become jealous or envious. They may say, "Who do they think they are doing XYZ?" To combat their negative response, remember this:

Act boldly and unforeseen forces will come to your aid.

Something magical happens when we move forward with force and intense desire. It's as if the universe around us bends to our will to make things manifest to support what we intend. It's like watching gravity in action, except we can't yet explain all the physics behind it. We just know that the end result is that the one who made those bold moves left others scratching their heads in disbelief.

If you are talking about true innovation, your path by definition requires there be naysayers and skeptics coming out of the woodwork. Again, study history and you'll discover that Einstein was considered to be of only average intelligence. Louis Pasteur was considered in his early years to be "nuts." Yet, they forged ahead boldly to realize their vision and defied their critics in the process. I recently watched a biography of Hugh Hefner, founder of *Playboy*. Whatever your views on the magazine, you have to admire his guts and vision amid all the skeptics. In one telling interview early on with Mike Wallace, Hefner was getting bombarded with accusations about *Playboy* being lurid and salacious. Hefner claims that during a commercial break Wallace leaned over to him and said, "You'll be doing something else in two years." And Hefner, the one who acted boldly, proved him wrong.

Lesson # 7—Leadership, fast, now: How to create momentum in the first days of starting something new

Starting with the first FDR administration during the Great Depression, there has been a yardstick by which every president is measured: What did I get done in the first 100 days? Bill Clinton was criticized for starting out unfocused in his first administration but showed dramatic improvement in his second administration. Study great leaders and you will see a propensity to make a statement early on about getting things moving quickly. This tradition underscores the importance of "getting started on the right foot" and not waiting too long to act.

When we decide to tackle something new or embark on a new course, it's best to really launch ourselves forward in a way that makes a splash and establishes momentum. Have you ever watched Olympic gold medalist Michael Phelps in a race right after the starting gun? He puts so much into that initial surge that the momentum seems to carry him halfway across the length of the pool before he actually starts swimming. And what starts out as a leading position stays that way throughout the race. When a firm enters the marketplace with an innovative new product, it is often considered to have "first mover" status, which means they are leading the way and have added momentum right off the bat. When you are starting something new, here are some "best practices" to help make you more successful from the get go.

Have some idea of what success looks like. I read once that if you don't know where you are going, any road will take you there. Every success starts with a vision. If you are leading a group of people at work, in your community or at home, make sure to clearly articulate where you are taking them and why. This is why the development of a mission statement is such an important exercise. In my work with financial advisor teams, one of the first things I do is interview each team member individually and ask them all the same question: What is the team trying to accomplish? Invariably, I will get different answers from each one. When we get together and I share the answers as a group, the leaders are upset at the team members for not knowing the answer. Yet, this is a leadership issue and thus starts at the top. Ideally, the most effective approach to developing a mission statement is to actually get the whole team involved in the statement creation process. If this is not practical, at least make sure that everyone is clear on your mission so they are at least "singing from the same hymnal."

Keep in mind that labels stick. Be deliberate and thoughtful before you label yourself or your product or service from the start because it's true that labels stick. When I worked in a home-office structure, I found it amazing that many in relatively high positions still called the financial advisors "brokers." Can everyone remember that commercial during the dot-com boom from a certain "discount broker" where the client is washing his boat while lamenting, "Broker? I'll tell you the only one who is broker. It's me . . ." This term has been a pejorative term for some time now in the field with advisors and clients alike. Most advisors now have the CFP designation or at least take a more holistic approach than is implied by the term broker. When you are thinking about what you are going to name something or somebody, make sure it's consistent with what you are trying to accomplish. When somebody asks, "What do you do for a living?" how do you answer? When you introduce yourself to a business prospect, what do you say?

Don't get caught spinning your tires. One momentum killer is getting stuck on a single issue or problem at the expense of moving forward with other items on your agenda. Presidents know that it's unlikely they will get all the items on their agenda completed, so it's important to prioritize. Don't adopt an all-or-nothing mindset. Be prepared to look at your first 100 days for what it is and what it is not. It is a beginning where mistakes will be made and lessons learned. It does not mean that you can't take a different course later if things don't work out as you intend. Life is a lot like a baseball game except you are the umpire and there is an unlimited number of times you can take a swing. And you are the only one who can call yourself out.

Wow, that was fast . . . If you want to know how to move into the passing lane of life, get things done for others fast. If you were to ask top executives to rank the qualities they most look for in a new hire, at the top of the list would be to have a sense of urgency in whatever project you are working on. Are you old enough to remember the old *Star Trek* series when Captain Kirk would ask the ship's engineer Scotty, "How much time do you need?" Inevitably Scotty would give him an estimate and proceed to beat it. When you get the reputation for doing things fast, you will be given more business, more responsibility and ultimately you will be paid more money. Are you looking for a way to boost your value in any situation? Set expectations of one timeline and then proceed to beat it. When it comes to business, think FedEx, not the post office. That's another great way to establish momentum right from the start in any business situation.

6

The Upside of Downside:
How to Take Advantage of Adversity

It's hard to have perspective if you've just lost your job or your business is way down and the bills are piling up. We're all more vulnerable to the pervasive negative news and the stresses that come during uncertain times. Change often brings more change as adjustments in the economy tear apart the fabric of families and communities alike. We hear horror stories of people losing their homes, collecting unemployment, moving back in with their folks. But in my research of booms and busts throughout history, I've discovered that not only are there survivors, there are people who actually would not have been nearly as successful *without* the tough times. In other words, many of their major successes didn't happen *despite* the tough times but *because* of the tough times. In following *The Undaunted Life,* they truly learned how to thrive in adversity. So can you!

SECRETS OF FORTUNE MAKERS: WHAT NOBODY TELLS YOU ABOUT TOUGH TIMES

There is a beautiful visitors' attraction in Richmond, Virginia, called Maymont. And the history behind it is even more colorful than the grounds in springtime. During the Gilded Age, a young attorney and Confederate war veteran named James Dooley became a "Captain of Industry" during the reconstruction of the south after the war. There is a museum to commemorate the era and what life was like for this young

tycoon and his family. Known as a brilliant legal mind, shrewd busi-
nessman and talented orator, Dooley would prove to be one of the most
successful leaders of his time. In hindsight, it's easy to see why being an
industrialist then would be so lucrative. But it's important to realize the
context of his rise to the top.

Imagine waking up one day with the realization that everything you
knew had changed. There are foreign troops occupying your town. You
had served time as a wounded prisoner of war and now realize you
fought for the losing side. The president of your country is now a run-
away fugitive. You've been labeled a loser. Even the currency in your
wallet is suddenly worthless. Your future seems completely out of your
hands. Others around you are dejected, despondent, mourning for a
lost cause, a dying way of life. Yet for some reason, you emerge from the
debris with a vision for the future. You can see something others can't.
James Dooley saw a need in this wreckage—the need to rebuild the
post-war south. History would show us that Dooley was a very ambitious visionary with a remarkable ability to set and achieve goals.

One of the most intriguing historical artifacts found buried in James
Dooley's personal items was his Latin dictionary. When he was 14 years
old, Dooley wrote the following on the inside cover, "When I have
$5,178,360, I will stop making money." He also scribbled down interest
calculations on this sum, apparently to determine how much interest
income this amount might generate. Talk about early retirement planning! Nobody knows where that exact figure came from or exactly what
drove him to write it but there are a few success lessons we can learn
from James Dooley.

Think big. In today's dollars Dooley's sum would be more like
$100,000,000 plus. This was an extraordinarily ambitious boy. And there
weren't exactly many success books on the market back then. How many
adults do you know who even bother to write down their goals? How
many 14 year olds? He then proceeded to make specific calculations to
determine his future income, as if he already had the money.

"What" comes before "how." There was no evidence that he had any
clue as to exactly how he was going to accumulate this amount. The

point is that he first established the end result—somehow instinctively knowing that the "how" would come to him later. And it surely did.

Wealth helps others. At Dooley's death in 1922, his estate minus his vast real estate holdings was estimated to be over $6,000,000 (that's six million dollars). And he gave half his fortune to the St. Joseph orphanage. At the time, this bequest was the largest single donation to a Catholic charity in U.S. history. The United States is the most generous nation in the history of the world—we give more to charity than the rest of the world. The reason we can do this is because we are a wealthy nation. There is honor in pursuing wealth. It is the pursuit of wealth that has produced a standard of living never before seen in the history of the world. It has become popular lately to demonize wealth and greed and label free-market capitalism as corrupt. We can all learn from the mistakes made in every boom/bust cycle; but don't make the mistake of thinking that somehow there is a better system than ours out there. There isn't.

Napoleon Hill once wrote that "within every failure are planted the seeds of equal or greater success." It's considered politically incorrect to talk about opportunities when everyone is hurting from a bad economy. But here are a few secrets that the highly successful know but won't come right out and tell you.

Seizing on needs

You just saw an example of a success after the bloodiest conflict in history, the Civil War. Look at what emerged after World War I. How about World War II? Because of all the death and destruction, there was a pent-up demand to rebuild with a shrunken labor pool. Also, if you saw the documentary *Supersize Me,* you know that fortunes have been made selling us things that appeal to a weakness or even ultimately kill us. The list is long. Consider the following industries based on addictions of one kind or another:

> *Casinos*—gambling addiction
> *Fast food*—obesity, diabetes, heart disease, cancer
> *Sugar and high-fructose corn syrup*

Caffeine—stress and sleep disorders
Tobacco—cancer, heart disease
Pornography—addictions
Women's media—eating disorders
Pharmaceuticals treating symptoms not causes—psychological dependencies

By no means am I condoning any of these industries. But the point is, when we believe there is a potential upside to any downside, we can direct our Inner Hero to creatively respond in a successful way.

Uncertainty is your friend

If you wait until the coast is all clear, rest assured you will pay a hefty premium. Whether you are talking about investments or entering a new career, by the time its appeal is obvious to everyone else, it's likely no longer as attractive. Supply and demand determines the price of everything, so you should time your moves in anticipation of what will happen, not in response to what is happening now. If you want to know the upside of something, ask yourself how much certainty there is in the outcome. The money manager Ken Fisher in his book, *The Only Three Questions that Count,* says that it's only by knowing what others don't that gives you an edge in investing.

The same could be said about most things we pursue. We all crave certainty, yet it's the lack of certainty that opens the door for new opportunities. Think about the best client or customer of your biggest competitor. When will you likely have a crack at getting that business? It's not when things are going good. But when you see uncertainty of any kind come into play, doubts begin to crop up and suddenly they are open to a second opinion. Many companies have gained enormous market shares during downturns because there are new questions about existing products or services. Do you remember the Tylenol scare a number of years ago when other pain relievers gained market share? What about when Coca-Cola changed their formula and came out with "New Coke?" Suddenly, that uncertainty around the original caused a surge in demand for the original.

Security is a myth. Did you base your career choice on the size of a company or how long they've been in business? Historically, these were important considerations, but in a rapidly changing economy it's best to place your security in your own skill set. The days of working for the same company for 40 years and getting a gold watch at retirement are fading into the sunset along with fax machines and phone booths. You are better off thinking of yourself as a contractor of services even if you work for another company. That way you have the right mindset to keep your options open when things get tight. Also, have you stayed with a job just because of the benefits package or the pension payout at retirement? Look what happened in Detroit, or with banks. There is a paradox in pursuing "security"—the more perceived security, the less real security. Peace of mind comes from confidence in your value, not from external validation from an entity.

Once we had a nanny leave our family because a national day care center offered her a job with slightly more pay, some health benefits and a 401k. Even though she was happy with us, she felt this center offered more long-term security. We told her that she would make more with us in 12 months and agreed to offer her health care coverage, but she left anyway. When we spoke with her later, it was clear that she would have been happier and ironically had more pay and benefits had she stuck it out with us.

EXTREME MAKEOVER: IF YOU CAN'T GO TO WORK, GO TO WORK ON YOURSELF

One of the upsides to going through tough times is that it gives you a rare opportunity to make big changes in yourself. Like that TV program where a crew comes in to make radical home improvements, a rough time in your business or life situation may be the perfect time for your own personal makeover. If you are out of work or in career transition, or dealing with an illness or disability, or adjusting to being newly retired or semi-retired, appreciate the fact that you can ditch all that old furniture and finally strip off that old paint. In essence, you can start fresh with an entirely fresh mindset. You have a clean slate, a chance to begin again, an opportunity to give birth to a new way of looking at yourself. Here are some questions to empower you to use this period as a time to shed that dead skin and breathe anew.

- Who were the people who really bugged you in your old work environment whom you no longer have to deal with?

- What work tasks did you hate at your old position that you no longer have to do?

- How could you use this time to improve your physical body?

- Are there aspects to your character you would like to improve?

- When was the last time you allowed your true personality to shine through?

- Have you lost your sense of humor over the years? How can you get it back?

- When was the last time you took some time to nurture yourself?

- Where have you always wanted to travel but have never been?

- Have you developed poor eating habits because of your hectic work schedule?

- Is it time to make some new friends?

- What interests and talents have you repressed because of your old job or old responsibilities?

- Who have you always wanted to be like or what have you always wanted to do but felt it was always "unrealistic?"

- What hobbies have you not pursued in years but now might pick up again?

- What old friends have you lost touch with whom you now have the time to reconnect with?

- What are you doing to counter the stress of being out of work?

- Is there a religion or faith that you can rediscover?

- What can you do for your immediate family that you didn't have the time to do before?

Let's imagine a typical scenario of someone ready for an extreme makeover. Jim, who is 50, just got laid off from his job of 15 years. He's 30 pounds overweight. He has started to drink more to medicate his feelings of depression and inadequacy, which of course is making things worse. He has begun to lose his temper more easily and frequently. His marriage is strained from the added stress, and the relationship with his two teenage kids is even more distant than before. His spiritual life is lacking. He realizes that he hasn't cultivated any new friends in years—he's been too busy with work and family. He just got word that a favorite uncle is seriously ill. His father has passed away and his mother is showing signs of dementia. College tuition expenses loom as his oldest kid is already a junior in high school. His retirement savings have been cut in half from a bear market.

Jim is spending the bulk of his time looking for new work. But as a coach working with Jim, I would suggest to him that there is no point in providing guidance on the business front with such glaring weaknesses on the personal front. It's like having your foot on the accelerator and the brake at the same time—even with the pedal to the metal, his wheels spinning, he's not really going anywhere. And by the way, what's the point if he gets somewhere but leaves all his family passengers behind?

5 SUGGESTIONS FOR ONE PERSON'S MAKEOVER

1. Get a physical

Have you ever known someone who discovered a life-threatening illness too late to cure? If only they had seen a doctor sooner. This happened in our family a few years ago when my wife's uncle complained of a pain in his rib cage. His excuse for not going to the doctor was he didn't have health insurance. He was diagnosed with myeloma cancer and given three to five years to live. Had they caught it sooner, the odds are they could have dramatically extended his life span. So we know that Jim needs to start with his own vitality first. He should immediately schedule an annual physical. He's at an age where prostate issues, high blood pressure and other problems can become life threatening quickly if left unchecked. At the same time, these are medical issues that can be effectively treated if discovered early enough. It would give Jim some numbers to work toward regarding weight, blood sugar levels, cholesterol levels, etc.

2. Adopt better nutrition habits

As we mentioned earlier about food consumption, Jim needs to get educated on how his eating habits are impacting his energy levels, which in turn impacts everything in his life. There is more information from books and seminars today than ever before on this subject. Jim should beware of "diets" and instead focus on real eating habit changes. Reducing sugar, salt, fat, processed foods, preservatives, caffeine and alcohol would be a start. Vitamin supplements should also be considered. If your doctor is not up to speed on the latest in prevention, look for another doctor. The fact is that most medical doctors are trained in how to cure disease but not necessarily prevent disease. I have a niece graduating from medical school and I asked her a simple question: Are they teaching you anything about prevention? It turns out that the entire curriculum is focused on what to do when a patient walks in sick. But by then, the disease has already been hard at work for a long time. It's not just closing the barn door after the horse is out, it's more like they find ways to get on the horse and slow it down. There is a huge medical establishment that is also big business.

The other day, I noticed a brand new medical building going up in our community with an enormous sign, "Heart Institute." At first glance you might say, "That's great, I know there is treatment if I ever have a heart attack." But then I realized that, like any for-profit business, they go where they can find the most customers, and there is an obesity problem here in Virginia. This new business is a reminder that we need to address the root causes of heart problems not just the treatment after the heart attack has already happened.

3. Exercise

Again, going back to our discussion about building physical energy in chapter 3, Jim needs to establish an exercise ritual of some kind starting with aerobic activity to begin shedding some pounds. He should start out slowly at first and work up to 30 minutes per day for a minimum of three to four days per week. Strength training is underrated by some, but at Jim's age it really is "use it or lose it." Muscles shrink with age, so it's vital to get all the major muscle groups moving. The leg muscles are the largest in the body, so you can burn the most calories using those. It's also a great way to release toxins in the body as muscle contraction massages our internal parts in a way that nothing else can. Having worked in a health club as a personal trainer, my recommendation is to keep changing your routines so your muscles don't get too used to certain motions coming in sequence. This can boost your results fast.

4. Address personal relationships

Our relationships are foundational. They comprise the reasons we want to make a living. We want to provide for our families. It's been said that when we are on our deathbed, the last thing we think about is our work. Our real legacy is our relationships, and the older we get the more important this becomes. What is the point in making a ton of money if we lose the love and respect of those we care about most? For Jim, this starts with his wife. He needs to set aside time each day to tune into her life. It's extremely stressful to be the spouse of someone out of work. He should find an inexpensive way to rekindle the romance: take walks together, meet for lunch, talk about something other than the economy, stock market or ball game.

5. Find a cause

Unemployment is far more debilitating to men than to women. Sorry ladies, but men are wired to be warriors and knights in shining armor. They hardly feel like Sir Lancelot when they are not relishing in battle victories or dragon slayings. So Jim needs to take a page out of John McCain's biography and find a cause greater than himself to become truly fulfilled. This may be the last thing on his mind, but it's a way to get out of himself and focus on others. It's also a way to combat feelings of depression. Lack of purpose when we get up every morning actually invites illness to our doorstep. Some areas to consider might be charity work, volunteer coaching, church work or community involvement.

SOMETIMES THE ANSWER IS RADICAL CHANGE

Have you ever made a major change and thought to yourself, "Wow, I should have done this years ago?" Well, sometimes change is the answer even if it means radical change. When we study success stories, we often find that the biggest turning points happen when something changes dramatically. As an American, I love stories of immigrants who come to this country and work hard to achieve the American dream. Sometimes they are famous people, sometimes not. Let me share one story about the not-famous type.

One day I was cold calling and I reached a Korean grocer in Atlanta by accident. The phone number I dialed was to another business but I miss-dialed by one digit and got him on the phone instead. His English was broken and hard to understand but somehow I managed to set an appointment to come see him. He gave me his address in an unfamiliar area. I pulled out my street directory and got some idea about where I was going and headed out.

As I exited off the bypass that surrounds the city, it didn't take me long to realize this was a rough neighborhood. It turns out that the Atlanta federal penitentiary was nearby and I actually heard gunfire as I nervously scanned street addresses looking for my prospect's store. When I reached the location, I initially chose to keep going. You see, his store was located next to a liquor store and there were seven or eight guys hanging out in the front holding brown bags sipping whatever was inside. Driving my little Honda Accord hatchback and wearing a white dress shirt and tie, I might as well have had a giant neon sign around my neck that read, "Hi, I realize I don't really belong here but please try to ignore me while I go about my business." I realized that part of staying out of harm's way was to avoid getting into harm's way in the first place. But another part of me said, "Wait a minute, am I really going to let a group of guys intimidate me into not going inside that store to see this prospect?"

So I shamed myself into doing a U-turn and entered the parking lot. Unfortunately, I quickly discovered that there was only one parking space available, and guess where? That's right, directly in front of these guys who looked like they had all served time in the prison down the road. My strategy was to get parked, avoid eye contact and move purposefully into my prospect's convenience store. As I got out of my car, I could feel every eye on me. But not a word was said. Inside, I was greeted by a clerk at the counter (later I found out this was his daughter) and was led to a back office. An unassuming man, quite short in stature, rose from his worn tattered office chair as I introduced myself. While he spoke in broken English, I was able to converse with him much better in person that I had over the phone. I asked him how he came to own the store and he proceeded to tell me his life story. His family managed to miraculously escape North Korea just before the start of the Korean War. His father was later killed in battle fighting for the South and his mother died years later of cancer. He described how tough it was on their family when his father died and he and his brother and sisters were barely able to survive on his mother's paltry wages. Still, he was grateful to have ended up on the South Korean side as many friends and family were still suffering under the oppressive regime of Jong Yung Ill. His father had shown great courage in leading his family across in spite of much criticism and fear.

He had come to the United States with his wife and kids just five years earlier and managed to start this business. Talk about being undaunted! He had saved an amazing $50,000 and was interested in learning how best to invest it. Despite only living in the States a relatively short amount of time, he was actually quite knowledgeable about finances. He was not afraid of the stock market but was more interested in mutual funds. When he asked if I had anything for him to read about them, I told him I had something in the car. When I walked out of the store, I went straight to my car. The gang was still there and all eyes were on me. I unlocked my door and reached into the back seat to open my briefcase and retrieve a brochure. As I was emerging from my car, I had the sinking feeling that somebody was right behind me. I was wrong—it wasn't "somebody," it was the whole gang. Brown bags in hand, they had formed a semi-circle around my car.

My heart rate accelerated and my adrenaline began to surge when the apparent leader of the group stepped toward me with a menacing stare and blurted out something that I didn't quite understand. I got the message anyway: I should not be here and they were going to kill me! What should I do? Well, when I was a kid I learned that dogs could literally smell fear and that, if they smelled fear, they had a predatory response to attack. So even though I was terrified on the inside, I looked directly into the eyes of the leader. Without saying a word, I acknowledged him and what he said, but dismissed the threat. Somehow it worked!

When I returned to my prospect's office I told him about the thugs and suggested we call the police. He looked puzzled. To him, this was no big deal. He probably would have reacted the same way later when the gang leader spit on my shoes before I drove off. I guess for a man who had seen war, this was a walk in the park. He eventually became a good client, but that was the last time I ever went to his shop. Many times, however, I stopped to appreciate how this man had endured and even initiated radical changes in his life to improve his situation. He had to flee in fear from his hometown, overcome the tragic early death of his father, move his new family to a new country, learn a new language, start a new business and become self-educated about money. All of this change with a spirit of curiosity and acceptance. We all can learn from such acts of courage.

FRESH STARTS

If you have ever been to the Palm Desert California area you've already experienced what I'm about to describe. The mountains there rise majestically from the sand floor and cast glorious shadows over the valley when the sun sets. It's fascinating to see how these shadows radically change in shape with the seasons. Depending on the sun's seasonal position, the landscape can look radically different and thus provides constant variety depending on the vantage point of the onlooker. And in the summer time, when it reaches 120 degrees, those shadows can provide much needed relief from the heat. Everything that faces the sun casts such a shadow, whether it's a palm tree or a person. It's part of the landscape. The shadows add to the overall beauty and charm of the desert. And if you think about shadows as those parts of our experience we would like to forget, remember that everything we do casts a shadow.

Every action has a consequence—some residual impact. We can no more separate that cause-and-effect relationship than we can separate a shadow from the object that produces it. But we don't have to focus on it unless we find beauty there. If we find pain, we can rely on the sun coming up again tomorrow and the promise of change. We can count on the seasons to cast new light on the subject and on our own lives.

Sometimes change comes in the form of a fresh start. When I was living in the desert, it was common to meet people who had moved there after something traumatic in their life. The desert can have a healing quality. Have you ever gone through a serious illness, a divorce or the death of a family member? Sometimes these events lead us to ponder extreme change in where we live and work. The desert was that kind of place. The summer heat can melt away even the most debilitating wounds. So don't underestimate the value of change just for change's sake.

I used to see this whenever I noticed one of my financial advisors in a rut. Sometimes I would orchestrate an office change to get them physically moving and break up their usual pattern of thinking. Have you noticed that when you go to certain places physically, your state changes immediately? It might be your childhood home, or a vacation spot; and the reaction could be positive or negative depending on your association with the place. If you have fond memories, you might find yourself having positive feelings. But if you have negative memories, you might find yourself feeling sad and not even knowing why. Though many years have passed since I went through the rigors and excitement of a new football season, to this day when I smell fresh-cut grass like the kind you will find on any college football field, I get simultaneously excited and nauseous! I remember both the adrenaline rush from the games and the pain from those summer two-a-day practices.

Moving to a new geographic area is something to consider if you have suffered from any trauma or upheaval. Sometimes just leaving your hometown to spread your wings can energize and uplift you. When you don't have all the reminders of what you've lost staring at you in the face, it can open the door to a new chapter in your life. This can also apply to your new job or career search. Perhaps overseas work might appeal to you, or investigating work that requires travel. It can accelerate your ability to move on and be more successful in the next phase of your life.

LOOK TWICE, DIG DEEPER

Of course there is a flip side to creating opportunities by making changes. Sometimes when we start searching for answers to improve our situation during tough times, we assume that we MUST look outside our own neck of the woods. But often if we will just look twice and dig deeper, we can find great opportunities right under our own noses. One of my favorite stories told by Earl Nightingale as well as Brian Tracy and others is called "Acres of Diamonds." There was an African farmer who heard stories of people striking it rich by discovering diamond mines. So he decided to sell his farm and begin his quest. After years passed without him finding a single diamond, he finally went back to his home village to see if he could get work on his old farm. When he returned he received shocking news: the person who bought his farm had found diamonds on his old property and was now fabulously wealthy! The lesson was clear. Before you assume that you have to leave home, take a look at what's underneath you right now.

Here are some ideas for how you might uncover hidden opportunities under your nose when adversity hits you.

Easy come, easy forget. What skills do you have that you might be taking for granted because they come easily for you? It's human nature for us to underestimate the value of something that seems effortless. Yet, those very things often can propel us to higher levels of success. For example, you might be very good at working with computers or working with your hands or organizing people. And because you do that work so fast, it only takes a small part of your workday, leaving time to do other work that requires much more time and effort.

Work less, make more. What would happen if you devoted much more of your time to doing things you were naturally skilled at? What would happen to your personal productivity? What would happen to your stress level? How would it improve your outlook and mood?

Hurricane watch. Do you view problems as opportunities to shine? I heard a story recently about a guy named Ed Pierce who was the top editor of the *Miami Herald* starting in the 1940s. This old-fashioned newspaperman tells the story of how the paper had a recurring feature whereby they would take two whole pages and do a kind of "hurricane watch." This meant that they would lay out a map and predict weather patterns over the state of Florida. Once, after over 500,000 copies had already gone to print, it was discovered that more than six cities had their names misspelled. Pierce, under pressure, decided to write an article challenging his readers to find all the misspelled cities. The reader who uncovered the most would be given a cash prize. The winner found over a dozen and Pierce later considered this move his most brilliant idea in over 40 years in journalism.

STAYING GRATEFUL FOR WHAT YOU HAVE

Tough times are a perfect opportunity to be grateful for what you still have. It puts things into perspective. During boom times we all take prosperity for granted and wants morph into needs. What are you thankful for even when things look bad in your outer world? Why not make a list of what you are grateful for as a reminder? Here are a few tips to get you started.

Health

If you still have your health you can work to rebuild what you might have lost in a downturn. I remember once a client inheriting millions, only to discover she had cancer with less than five years to live.

She received this diagnosis literally two weeks after the money hit her account as she was packing for a two-week European cruise. I recall one client who had scrimped and saved his entire life so that he and his wife could retire to their mountain home. After working for his company for 40 years, he had accumulated a sizable 401k that he was rolling over. We had an income plan put together that would allow he and his wife to do the traveling they had always dreamed about. Then one day I got the call from him. I could tell something was wrong by the despondent tone in his voice. His wife had just died of a sudden heart attack. All their retirement dreams vanished. All their sacrifice seemed in vain, as years of savings could not erase the pain of the loss of his life partner. It was a vivid reminder to be grateful for what you have because you never know when it can be taken away.

Family

We've always heard that it's vital to put our families first but ,when we are put to the test in challenging times, it means even more. Regardless of what happens to our business or career or portfolio, it's our family relationships that pull us through. Recently I attended a family reunion of my mother's side of the family where over 140 relatives showed up. We had to wear color-coded nametags so everyone could see what part of the family tree we were from. To be surrounded by all these people who cared about each other and had common roots was something I'll never forget. We heard stories about the Great Depression and how, when times were tough, the whole family pitched in to help. All my mother's brothers and sisters depended on each other during those days. They all supported each other financially when it was time to attend college—the older adult kids would send what they could to help pay tuition or living expenses.

So if you are facing a tough time, ask yourself if you are using this time to reconnect with estranged family members. Don't wait for funerals. Pick up the phone now or pay a long overdue visit. You might be surprised by what you learn and how much better you'll feel.

Keep perspective

We always think *we* have it tough when adversity comes. We forget how it has been for others. For example, do you appreciate how even a relatively poor person in our culture has a much better standard of living than even the richest kings 500 years ago? Or even 200 years ago? Thomas Jefferson's home, Monticello, is a special historical place to visit in Virginia. If you are ever in the area, I strongly suggest you take a tour of the home and grounds. Here are some things that will jump out at you to give you a sense of just how far we've come since the founding of our country.

Indoor heating. Even most people of low income have indoor heating, yet in Jefferson's day, there were fireplaces everywhere and it took a lot of wood and labor to keep the house warm.

Air conditioning. Virginia summers can get pretty hot and humid. Shade trees offered relief by day in those days, but in the nighttime they relied on open doors and windows and prayed for breezes.

Bugs. If you live in a hot and humid climate you know about the kind of insects that literally come out of the woodwork in the summer. They range from pesky mosquitoes to old-fashioned cockroaches. Most Americans have sprays and treatments that handle them. Imagine what it must have been like without that?

Indoor toilets. We've taken a tour of the grounds several times, and on one visit the guide made sure we all knew where Thomas Jefferson used the bathroom most frequently. He showed us the "outhouse" area away from the house under one of the terraces and proceeded to explain things about the early 19th century elimination experience that I won't repeat here. Let's just say that even the upper crust of society had it much worse than the average citizen today in this department.

Clean, indoor water. It's one thing to have to go outside to use the bathroom, but how about having to bring water in from a well by the bucketful to wash dishes or take a bath? Granted the Romans had some pretty cool indoor plumbing technology, but in America at that time, there was no such thing even for the wealthiest folks. And if you wanted a hot bath, you had to heat the water over a fire first.

Clean water demanded new freshwater wells be dug periodically, a far cry from our world of convenience stores with 10 selections of bottled water.

Refrigeration. When it comes to food preservation, we've probably gone overboard with all the preservatives and chemicals in our food. But keeping things cool happens to be the way to keep foods fresh. How many of us could handle not having a refrigerator? Meat was cured with sugar or salt back then and there were no refrigerated trucks to bring in dairy products or produce. You ate whatever you could grow or trade with your neighbors.

Ice. It was fascinating to learn all the things Jefferson brought back from his travels to France. You've probably heard he loved French wines. But what you may not know is that he also discovered "ice cream" while there. This delicacy was all the rage and for good reason. You had to be able to have ice to have ice cream but the only ice was the kind formed in the winter, compliments of Mother Nature. Jefferson had a special pit made under one of his terraces and lined it with stones. Then ice was placed in the pit during the winter so as to be available in the spring and summer. Guests of the estate were truly delighted if they were ever so privileged to get to taste this special new treat.

Electricity. Can you imagine having to rely on "candle power" to light a room or get around after dark? How many of us take electrical power for granted? Ben Franklin is known to have discovered electricity in this era but its generation and application would have to wait until Thomas Edison came on the scene. Heating, cooling, water pumps, light bulbs, etc., all depend on that magic current.

Communication. In the age of cell phones, BlackBerrys and the Internet, it's easy to forget that in Jefferson's day, before the telegraph, messages were carried mainly by foot or on horseback. The idea of instantaneous conversations across vast distances was mindboggling. Next time you are on a cell phone watching the Super Bowl and blogging on the Internet, relish the moment, enjoying the miracle of the airwaves.

Transportation. We all know about the horse-and-buggy days, but next time you are on that plane consider that we cross distances in minutes that used to take days and even weeks. We are able to go places that our ancestors only dreamed about going. Jefferson's trip "across the pond" on ship would leave today's average traveler nauseous five minutes after leaving port. There was even real risk of not even making it if the wrong weather pattern emerged.

Medical care. If you look at the average life-span back in Jefferson's day, his 83 years was actually quite astounding. Like a fire sweeping through a field of grass, diseases like smallpox, malaria, diphtheria, pneumonia and countless others spread unabated in those days without hope for cure. Jefferson not only outlived his beloved wife Martha, he also outlived many of his children and grandchildren. When it comes to the history of disease, can you imagine what it must have been like to be afraid of catching so many incurable things? Next time you are in a doctor's office, pay tribute to the advances in medicine that give you relative confidence that most of the diseases you might catch either have cures or at least treatments.

If you need more recent evidence of the changes we take for granted, turn the clock back only about 100 years. Here are some U.S. statistics for the year 1907:

- Only 14 percent of the homes in the U.S. had a bathtub.

- Only 8 percent of the homes had a telephone.

- A three-minute call from Denver to New York City cost 11 dollars.

- There were only 8,000 cars in the U.S. and only 144 miles of paved roads, and the maximum speed limit in most cities was 10 mph.

- The average U.S. worker made between $200 and $400 per year.

- More than 95 percent of all births in the U.S. took place at HOME.

- 99 percent of all U.S. doctors had NO COLLEGE EDUCATION! Instead, they attended so-called medical schools, many of which were condemned in the press AND by the government as "substandard."

- Sugar cost 4 cents a pound, eggs 14 cents a dozen and coffee 15 cents a pound.

- Most women only washed their hair once a month and used Borax or egg yolks for shampoo.

- There was no Mother's Day or Father's Day.

- Only 6 percent of all Americans had graduated from high school, and two out of every ten adults could not read or write.

LESSONS FROM THE ADVENTURE TRAIL

When we experience any sort of adversity in our lives, we tend to examine new directions and new possibilities. We think about alternative paths. We keep our options open. We consider choices that may have sounded "crazy" or not consistent with things we've done in the past. But as we get older there is a tendency to believe there is something to the saying "you can't teach an old dog new tricks." Actually, you can. Challenging times can also be times of great discovery and growth if we are not afraid to step in and be vulnerable. I had an experience of this not long ago, and I'd like to pass along these lessons I learned then.

1. Old dogs can learn new tricks—on the right horse

Colorado is one of my favorite places in the world and my wife has family in the Durango area. We visit there any chance we get. In the winter, there is the Durango Mountain Ski Resort, a hidden treasure for crowd-weary vacationers, and the summers offer a wide range of outdoor activities. We enjoy breathing in the crisp fresh air, viewing the majestic Rocky Mountains, whitewater rafting, hiking and being around the down-to-earth folks we find there.

During one visit, my wife's dad, one of the most fun-loving human beings I've ever known, arranged an amazing adventure for us apart from our young children that was a first for both of us. He put together a four-day, three-night back country horse trek in the pristine Chicago basin area north of Durango. My wife grew up around horses and even trained champion show horses, but I had never spent that much time in the saddle. And my idea of rustic camping is when you have to leave the motor home to use the campsite bathroom. But I was not going to show any signs of being a city slicker.

So we arrived at the rendezvous point where each of us was introduced to the horse we would be riding over the next four days. Part of the pre-trip process involved letting the trail ride leader know our level of experience with horses. I soon discovered that there are advantages to being the rookie that far outweigh the disadvantages. I was given the strongest, most experienced trail horse. I was also given extra pointers and tips from the start.

2. Take charge even when you don't know how

My horse's name was Jack and he could walk that trail blindfolded. His only vice was a propensity to want to eat anything and everything on the way. His appetite matched his size and I was instructed to "keep yanking the reins" each time he over-indulged on daises, dandelions or tall grass. The leader told me that it was critical to establish control early with this big animal because if I didn't he would fight me at every turn for the rest of the ride. When it comes to horses I learned that you have to take charge even though you don't really know how. Like a car with a sensitive gearshift my horse responded to even the slightest command to change directions. But I kept listening and taking instruction from the trail boss and I started to get the hang of it.

3. Know when to delegate and let go

My first big challenge came as we approached our first steep hill. I was instructed beforehand to "lean forward in my saddle and shift my weight and stirrup positioning so that I was helping Jack climb." At first it was awkward because you must balance that sense that you are in control with that need to let go and just go with the flow. There were times on that ride when I had to let the horse do what he knew how to do and get out of the way. Sure enough, as I focused on each step the horse made, I began to appreciate how all those micro decisions about hoof placement depending on the terrain was best left to him.

How could I possibly control everything? It was counterproductive to even try.

Do you find yourself not trusting others to do things to help you in a new venture or direction? It's fundamental to your success to surround yourself with people you trust and let them do their job to help you along your new path. Like the country song by Kenny Rogers about the poker game of life, "You have to know when to hold 'em, know when to fold 'em, know when to walk away and know when to run . . ."

4. Sometimes you just have to learn by doing it

When was the last time you were challenged to acquire a new skill? How long do you research or think about it before actually doing it? Are you someone who likes to learn by reading about things first? Or talking about it for hours before taking action? It's vital to remember that sometimes you just have to learn by doing, and the sooner the better.

After we climbed our first big incline, it was time to experience my first major "decline." Going down a steep decline on a horse actually requires a lot of skill. And it's very scary if you've never done it. The truth is that someone of my existing skill level had no business even trying it. I was nearly thrown off my horse several times before the trail boss realized what was going on and gave me some spot coaching to solve the problem. I was not positioned properly in the saddle. I was not putting my feet out far enough out in front of the horse. I was not holding the reins right or moving in the right rhythm to match the horse's movements. This is when I suddenly realized that I needed to imagine doing the limbo—leaning back much further, where I could almost feel my back touching the rear of the house as we went down that steep decline. When we reached a temporary bottom, I shouted out "Yes!" I had just passed my first skill test and would be much more confident going forward.

5. Believe that scary can be fun

The more time I spent in the saddle, the more confident I became. I learned how to really steer my horse. I even mastered how to hold the reins with one hand while knocking down tree limb obstructions with the other. I could speed up to a trot and put on the brakes with proper pressure at will. I knew when to just let Jack eat as we went and when to keep him moving along so we didn't get behind. But just when I was feeling pretty good about my progress along came a real test of nerves. At my father-in-law's suggestion, the trail boss led us to a spectacular vista above the snow line. This was August so most of the snow had melted, but there were parts at high altitude where we actually went through some snow. When we came around a bend, we were awestruck. Not a word was spoken, just that familiar sound of horses' hooves moving us all closer and closer to the edge.

Then our trail boss told us we were going down to another spot below, with even better views of the mountains and valley. The problem was I could not even see the path—it was all rocks with no visible trail. As we started out, the steepness brought on instant and overwhelming vertigo as Jack meandered down one hoof at a time. Then, from another horse and rider in the group, I heard the dreaded sound of gravel moving downhill—that shifting, tumbling, crackling sound of the ground giving way under the weight of a 1,500 pound animal. Trying to focus on the scenic beauty, I said to myself, "Well, if this is how I go, it's one hell of a way to go." Somehow we made it to a "shelf" area where we enjoyed lunch with a surreal view. On our way down we had to make our way down a trail that came dangerously close to a huge waterfall— one false move and both Jack and I would fall to our deaths. But as we went around a hairpin curve, I felt like I was suspended in midair, high above this gushing body of water, and a rush of euphoria overcame my fear. Like a roller coaster ride at the park, I was able to turn my fear into just plain fun. I was having a blast.

It was a dramatic reminder of that fine line between scary and fun. Like horror movies and roller coasters, this ride became a scary moment that I would fondly speak of later. Think about that for a moment in your own life. When you encounter something new that scares you, can you develop a sense of adventure and childlike wonder about it?

6. Know the horse you're riding

On this trail excursion, one of the things I learned was that horses are a lot like people. They each have a different personality type. As I got to know Jack, my horse on this adventure, it became clear that Jack was different than the other horses. He was a bit anti-social and got very irritated with other horses if they got near him. Whenever he was taking a drink from the creek, he would go to great lengths not to be too near the other horses. But as I bonded with Jack we developed an understanding: as long as he agreed not to try to buck me out of my saddle, I would agree to do everything I could to help him help me get to the next stop. I praised him, pet him, etc. Have you ever seen someone get obnoxious with a waiter or food person? Are they nuts?

The lesson here is clear: take the time to do some introspection on your own personality, and also take the time to understand the personalities around you. Come to your own understanding when dealing with others and you'll get more cooperation.

7. Competition improves performance

Jack was competitive. Whenever another horse came up from behind and began to pass him, he kicked into another gear. Granted it was a bit irritating, but to see that instinct in action was interesting. I'm a big fan of the story of the race horse Seabiscuit and how he had the ability to really accelerate when coming from behind or when another horse threatened his lead.

Are you naturally competitive? There is a new movement in some circles to challenge the value of competition, but we can all see that in the most competitive arenas you get the best overall performance. Does somebody really think that the Olympics would be the same if everybody got a gold metal? Talk with any athlete and they will tell you that their best performances weren't just about beating their best time—it was about winning the race. You don't need to be obsessed with the competition. Instead, use competition as a way to elevate your game and bring out your best performance. Just ask Jack.

DO WHAT YOU LOVE NOW

If times are tough, we might as well do what we love, right? When trouble comes, rather than simply avoiding new pitfalls, we can practice thinking big. For example, when the economy is down, there is less "opportunity cost" in pursuing something else because you are giving up less. What most people don't realize is that a slow economy, a job loss or a financial setback might actually be the catalyst to listen to your heart. You've heard the expression "starving artist," right? Well, when you are going to starve anyway, why not starve while you are doing something you're passionate about?

So what do you really want to be when you grow up? Have you been holding off because on the surface you seem to be doing so well? You are able to provide for your family. You are able to belong to that country club, go out to nice dinners, take those luxury vacations. But deep down, what would you really like to be doing? Here's a fact: we spend far more time at work and devote far more energy to our careers than on anything else. It's totally irrational that so many people hate their jobs. Obviously there are economic realities, but when you see all the layoffs, downsizing, outsourcing and business cycle disruptions, it's time to think long and hard about earning some "psychic income," especially when the differential is small compared to the real income.

BEWARE OF THE FUDS

So why do so many people hold back and never bother to actually do what they love to do? In my observation, it's usually one of three things: Fears, Uncertainties and Doubts. I call them the FUDS.

Fears

The biggest block is old-fashioned fear, and the most common form of fear is fear of the unknown, as in "I'm going to end up worse off than I am now." It's rational to only want change that makes us better off. But that's not what stops us. It's the fear of being worse off. One of the things I've really enjoyed about being a father is to watch what happens in childhood development. In the early years we see that kids are fearless, almost kamikaze in how they approach things. As parents, we are the ones terrified by the hazards of everyday life for our kids. Every household item from the frying pan to laundry detergent to a flight of stairs presents the possibility of imminent danger. I will never forget buying specially padded carpet for the bottom of our stairs in preparation for the day one of our kids would take a spill. Then one day it finally happened. We had some friends over and lost track of where our two-year-old daughter was playing. Suddenly, we heard a giant thud. You know how you can always gauge the level of disaster by how long it takes to hear the cry? The longer you have to wait the worse it is. But as long as you hear a cry you know they are still breathing! After we heard the "thud" we went running to the bottom of the stairs and wouldn't you know it? My wife had removed the carpet for this gathering to make room for a decoration piece. Luckily, our daughter survived with just a big knot on her head.

Fear is there to serve our basic survival instincts. It's hardwired in our being, but much of it is no longer useful once you move beyond physical danger. So it's our responsibility to move beyond fear in our lives so we can be free to choose our own destiny. It's not a matter of eliminating fear but channeling that emotion into power or focus or some other more positive emotional state. The other side of fear is confidence. It's all a matter of shaping and morphing those emotions so they work for you rather than against you as you try to live *The Undaunted Life* and achieve your goals.

Uncertainties

There is nothing more paralyzing than a lack of certainty. We are creatures of habit. We want to know what comes next because that's what gives us a sense of control. Uncertainty is akin to being out of control. The key during down times is to make sure you have an action orientation. It's like riding a bicycle: you will have a greater sense of control and balance when you are pedaling. Even if you are going in the wrong direction, it's better than sitting in place because when we do that we are raising the uncertainty meter. We are giving our subconscious mind the impression that we really don't know what we're doing, which leads to more uncertainty, and we have a downward spiral in the making. There's wisdom to the expression, "Lead, follow or get out of the way." It's the action orientation here that is the answer for greater control and the key to vanquishing those uncertainties.

Doubt

A close cousin to fear and uncertainty is doubt. We have doubt in our abilities, doubt in our choices, doubt in other people, doubt in the tools we use, doubt in the ultimate outcome. In many respects doubt is an absence of faith. Studies have proven that people who have a religious or spiritual faith lead happier and longer lives. Doubt is like a cancer that grows and creeps into your psyche if you are not careful to avoid it.

Have you ever watched what happens in a football game when the defense is able to rattle the quarterback early in a game? Or with a performer who seems to be having an off night? Have you ever seen a time-out being called before a field goal kick or a basketball free throw? The opposing coach wants that player to think about it. That's because the more we think about doing something, the more time is allowed for doubt to emerge.

Just as plants need water to grow, doubt needs negative thought patterns. Here are a few things to watch out for to make sure that doubt plant withers for lack of attention.

Negative people. When you are at the beginning stages of anything, be especially careful about the people you associate with. As motivational speaker Zig Ziglar says, "You can't fly with the eagles if you are scratching with the turkeys." These folks can shoot down a dream before it even gets on the launch pad. And sometimes it's not what they say but what they don't say, or the look they give you. If you have an ambitious plan that might put you in another category socially or financially, they may feel threatened by the possibility of your success. Don't be surprised if some people even withdraw as they learn about your plans.

Distractions. What happens when we take our eye off the ball— when our goals begin to compete with things that appear urgent but are really not that important? I'm talking about gossiping at the water cooler, watching too much television, getting bogged down in minutia. Steer clear of these hideouts where doubts can emerge.

Baggage. We all carry doubts based on our past. Picture someone carrying a bucket up a hill with one hand. As you noticed their heavy breathing, you would be tempted to ask, "Hey, why are you carrying that bucket?" It seems obvious to others but you've been carrying it around so long you don't even know it's there. Have you failed in the past but carry around shame from that experience? Did you grow up hearing "you can't?" Do you have a yoke or burden around some unresolved need from childhood? Are you an over-achiever driven by the need for approval from others because you never got it growing up? Are you an under-achiever because you desperately want to avoid criticism?

If you are aware of these seed plants for doubts, you can thwart them from growing.

WHAT DOESN'T KILL YOU MAKES YOU STRONGER

Yet another upside to downside is the simple fact that we grow through the experience of adversity. Tough times test our metal. What doesn't kill you makes you stronger, or, "The strongest steel is forged in the hottest flame." For example, if you were to see what is happening to your muscles during weight lifting, you would actually see muscle fibers tearing. Then they grow back larger in anticipation of having to handle that load again. This is necessary in order to expand the muscle's capabilities. It's the same when we go through adversity. If we are able to withstand the pressure of the load, we actually get stronger in the process.

The Marine Corps uses this concept in its training. They want to "break you" then "re-make" you, only this time as a strong fighting machine. They do this by subjecting new recruits to grueling training at Paris Island, South Carolina. I had a high school friend who went into the Marines right after graduation and he told me that they find a way to "break down" everybody—even those who seem to be doing everything right. My friend seemed to be breezing through without much friction, then one day, out of the blue, he was called over after exiting the shower and made to stand at attention near a door as the instructor proceeded to slam the door into his toe for no reason. He was making a point—he needed to be broken just like everyone else, even if he seemingly didn't really need it as much as the others.

CHANGE IS THE ONLY CONSTANT

Nature is full of examples of this principle at work. Evolution shows how animals respond to adversity. They simply evolve or become extinct over time. Anthropologists point out that surviving tribes passed on their genes because they were able to adapt to the changes. Scientists speculate that the dinosaurs vanished because they couldn't handle sudden climate change. Free-market capitalism is proof of this process at work in business. Take a look at this list and take a guess as to what they all have in common:

> Victor Talking Machine
> American Sugar Refining
> Nash Motors
> Curtis-Wright
> General Electric
> Texas Gulf Sulphur
> International Shoe
> Corn Products
> Esmark

Each was once one of the Dow 30 stocks in the Dow Jones industrial average. If you look at the Dow Jones industrial average today, how many of those companies do you think are still among the original 30? The answer is one—General Electric. All the others were either absorbed or driven out of business. The lesson here is that no matter how established a business, it's vulnerable to change. And no matter what you are doing today, it's a virtual certainty that you will be doing something different down the road.

Let's take my familiar world of the financial advisor. Below we can see the evolution that has accelerated among the very top advisors over the last 10 years.

From:	*To:*
Financial Product	Financial Planning
Clients Buy Something	Clients Buy Into Something (A Process)
Transaction Commissions	Asset Management and Advisory Fees
Salesmanship Orientation	Stewardship Orientation
Information Delivered	Wisdom Delivered
Individual Advisor	Advisor Teams
Investment Specialists	Total Wealth Management

Investors and their advisors have certainly gone through some extraordinarily tough times. When tough times hit an industry like this, you will begin to see new winners emerge and losers fade in market share. You can take a look at each dimension and see that the ones that have successfully transitioned and evolved are actually gaining in this environment.

Regardless of the industry you are now in or plan to be in, the dynamic of change is constant. And that is a healthy thing. Remember that we need obstacles and adversity. As Winston Churchill once said:

"Kites rise highest against the wind—not with it."

MAKING WAVES

If you buy into the concept that change is the only constant, then why not play a much larger role in that dynamic? It's become popular in our culture and in business books to attempt to "manage change," "respond to change," etc., the implication being that the best we can do is react to the changes as they come. I would argue that the most successful individuals and companies are doing much more than that. They are not just riding the waves, they are making the waves. If you have ever worked in a traditional corporate environment, you know that one of the surest ways to get fired is making too many waves—ruffling too many feathers as you try to implement changes. But the reality is that the most successful executives are stirring things up a bit. The mavericks are the ones challenging the status quo. They are thinking down the road and asking the questions: How can we get ahead of the curve? What should we be doing now that two years from now we wish we would have already done? That's the kind of preemptive strategic thinking that separates leaders from followers. It blazes new trails and explores new possibilities. It drives the innovation that is so necessary for the survival of cultures, companies and individuals. If you are trying to create an entirely new wave that you see turning into a real surfer's fantasy, it's likely your initial ride will be lonely. But take heart—eventually you'll hit the beach to the sound of cheering fans as others ask how they can do what you just did.

SOMEONE IS BUYING SWAMPLAND!

Can you imagine back in the 1950s what many were saying when they heard about a creative artist who wanted to create a theme park with rides named after cartoon characters? This seemed unimaginable to most and unfathomable at the time with existing technology. Yet one man was truly ahead of his time and dared to dream of something so compelling and so innovative that people and technology eventually came along for the ride. He sought change and went after it with a truly undaunted spirit, sticking with his dream despite conventional wisdom.

If you put yourself back in the early 1970s, can you imagine your reaction to news that somebody was buying up swampland in the middle of Florida? Would you think he was crazy or perhaps there was a grander vision in the making? After the success of Disneyland in California, Walt Disney's reputation as a visionary was already to a point where he was forced to use "shell companies" to buy the land that would eventually become Disney World in Orlando. Unfortunately he died before his vision was complete, but his legacy will live on for many generations.

When you feel like you are wading into murky waters surrounded by alligators and leaches, you need to keep your eye on the bigger picture. It's highly possible that you are way ahead of your critics, that you are a person ahead of your time, like Bill Gates or those young guys who launched GOOGLE. Even if you are facing some kind of adversity, let your imagination run wild. Don't let conventional thinking keep you so grounded that you let your dreams fade in the background. Use this time to create something.

TIME FOR TOTAL IMMERSION

If you find yourself out of work or exploring new possibilities, one huge upside is finally having the time to totally immerse yourself in learning something new. There is a powerful learning concept called "total immersion" that has been proven to accelerate the learning process of just about anything. We see this especially when learning foreign languages.

Have you ever seen the movie, *Groundhog Day,* with Bill Murray? In the movie, the lead character is a weatherman who gets stuck in a small town where he is to report whether the groundhog sees his shadow. Instead, he finds himself in a world where he awakens every morning to the old Sonny and Cher song, "I Got You Babe," and experiences a permanent deja vu—reliving the same events over and over again from the previous day. But what he soon realizes is that this new world has some advantages. He wants to win over the girl who is also his producer and uses each day to learn a little bit more about what she wants in a guy. Eventually he learns ice carving, French and even how to play jazz piano to impress his target. This pursuit of new skills finally culminates in "the perfect day" where he becomes the town hero. He's ultimately successful in getting the girl and the movie ends with the "next day" finally arriving with her in his arms, presumably to live happily ever after.

Soon after realizing what was happening, he sat in the bed-and-breakfast living room watching the same episode of *Jeopardy* with the other boarders, impressing everyone with his ability to answer every question. But as we see he gets bored quickly with that exercise. Then he finally sees the opportunity to indulge in something more productive and meaningful. At one point he even saves the life of a homeless man, shedding his arrogant nature to lend a hand to somebody in need.

To me, the most interesting premise of the movie was this idea that he could totally immerse himself in developing the perfect day. He could keep practicing, totally consumed by a goal—to get the girl. And because he wanted her so badly, he could take up a totally new project and master it because he had the luxury of time. So rather than take up a new project part-time or piecemeal, why not create your own Groundhog Day and totally immerse yourself in that project or skill you've been meaning to do but just never had the time to do it?

BLESSINGS IN DISGUISE

Have you ever had something bad, traumatic or super stressful happen to you, only to look back years later and discover feelings of appreciation for what happened? I remember living on the beautiful coast of southern California right on the ocean enjoying the sound of gentle waves hitting the shore and spectacular sunsets. Then over the course of a few months my world was completely turned upside down. When I was approached about running a branch office in the desert, I did not have a good initial feeling at all. My boss told me that there were more than 100 golf courses there at the time. Strike one—I was not a good golfer. Then he explained that it was sunny all year long. Strike two—I was already in paradise with no desire to leave. Then he told me "there was a very wealthy client demographic population there." Strike three—I was already surrounded by wealthy clients and besides, I was single, with no desire to move into "the land of the newly wed and nearly dead."

But despite the initial negatives, there was a charm to the area that is hard to explain if you've never been there. And after moving into my condo on a golf course with a "double-fairway view," I was in for quite an adventure. I met my wife there and made lifelong friendships. I fell in love with those desert evenings and the August clouds. Riding up on the tram and then hiking where the temperature is 40 degrees cooler in the summer was exhilarating. I enjoyed the outstanding restaurants and the laid-back desert lifestyle. Whenever I traveled back to L.A., I sighed with relief when I got back home. If you had told me just six months earlier that I would be happy living in a desert, I would have told you that you were crazy. In the most unlikely places, I found lots of joy and fun times. In hindsight, this move was a blessing in disguise.

What have you gone through or are going through that just might be a blessing in disguise? Are you open to the possibility that a rough patch might turn out to be "just what the doctor ordered?" If you can see any sign that any kind of current uncertainty or adversity is just some needed pause on your way to the top, you are well on your way to living *The Undaunted Life.*

Referral Rich™: 7 Steps to Leverage Who You Know

No matter what kind of work you do, building referrals is critical. And yet, so many people lack a basic strategy or understanding of what to do or what to say to gain the kind of referrals they need, in the numbers they need them. Why? I've grappled with that question for years through my advising, coaching and training, and I think I've found some answers. In response, I've developed a system of steps to help anyone become more undaunted, and far more successful, in attracting referrals. Would you like to become Referral Rich? Let's go right to the steps to see how.

STEP #1: WHY "WHO YOU KNOW" IS MORE IMPORTANT THAN "WHAT YOU KNOW"

The best way to understand this first step is through an illustration. A young intern named Mike was spending his summer between his junior and senior year at a large sales organization. He saw the cars some of the veteran sales people were driving and heard about the amount of money they made. Determined to learn how they were able to earn that much, he kept asking around about who the top salesperson was at the organization. It was a 30-year veteran of the firm named Harvey and, after some persistent requests, Harvey agreed to let Mike watch how he worked.

One morning, Mike meandered down the hall to Harvey's office and sheepishly knocked on the door. As Harvey instructed him to come in,

Mike was immediately intimidated by all the awards on the wall. There behind a stately looking mahogany desk was a distinguished gray-haired gentleman, impeccably dressed. He had that "silver fox" look of somebody who could star in a soap opera as a super-rich patriarch. Harvey began to engage the intern in some small talk when suddenly the phone rang. From hearing Harvey speak in the five-minute conversation, Mike figured he had just completed a rather sizable order. When he hung up, Mike asked him how much money he just made. Harvey did a quick calculation in his head and said, "About $10,000." Mike's jaw dropped. "You mean you just spent five minutes on the phone and made $10,000?" Harvey looked at him and said, "Yes, that conversation took five minutes, but the relationship with the person on the other end took me 20 years to build."

The lesson from this story is clear: ultimately what we get in life is going to come from what we give to other people—the value we provide others. It is people who make those buying decisions. It is people who make those hiring decisions. It is people who provide services. It is people who can become raving fans or the source of negative advertising. And ultimately, all our successes or failures will directly hinge on the contacts we establish, the relationships we build, the trust we earn over time.

We is bigger than me

There is only so much that any of us can accomplish as individuals. Without help from others, our influence and impact shrink. We all bring strengths and weaknesses to the table. And regardless of what you are trying to accomplish in your career, business or personal life, you can do it faster, easier and cheaper, and on a much bigger scale, when you have access to the right people.

At the core of being Referral Rich is the realization that in life "we is bigger than me."

When we study successful companies, organizations, countries and families, we see this holds true time and again. Let's take the founding of our nation as an example. Can you imagine a country without

George Washington, Thomas Jefferson or Ben Franklin? While each of these men were giants in their own right, it was only when they came together in a common cause that they became truly legendary. They could have just as easily ended up at the end of a rope, hung for treason. But they believed in something. They believed that this new, emerging country was something special—even worth dying for. They believed that united together this nation could achieve great things. They organized around an idea, a vision of what might be: that freedom could reign over tyranny, that the people could rule themselves. Did they carry that undaunted spirit? You bet. But, before they could trust that their vision would work, they first had to trust each other. Before they could get others to buy into this concept of modern democracy, they had to commit to it themselves.

When you think about referrals, it's more than just getting a name and a number so you can make a sale, get a new job, or get a better product or service. It's about seeing the connections, building a network, helping to improve the lives of everyone around you. And it's getting others excited and committed to helping you accomplish what you are trying to accomplish. The more you go about achieving your goals with an eye toward bringing others along for the ride, the more amplified your results.

Picture a pebble thrown into a lake and the ripple effect that spreads that energy well beyond the point of contact. This is the dynamic behind being Referral Rich. And of course the bigger the initial "splash" or impact, the wider and longer the resulting wave.

How big is your signal?

If you look at the ad dollars spent on a 30-second TV spot, you begin to appreciate how, when it comes to reaching people with your message, size and scale count. When these ads command six or even seven figures you might ask why would anybody pay that? The answer is the size of the audience. These messages reach hundreds of thousands of people, in some cases millions. It might be simple common sense, but it's easy to lose sight of the basics in an increasingly complex world. The fact is, the more people you know, the bigger your referral network and the larger your impact when you deliver any message.

Have you ever seen a broadcast signal tower? These base stations act as boosters to signals passed through the air. Think of your network of people as a way to boost your own signal. And the more powerful your signal, the bigger the audience you can influence. Have you ever been driving on the interstate and found yourself searching for local radio stations? You can always tell how strong the signal is by how far you can go before that signal fades. Obviously, the longer the station's audience is able to tune in, the more ad dollars they can command.

We see this in the world of job hunting. For example, let's compare two individuals, Susan and Mary, who are both actively looking for a new job in their chosen field of pharmaceutical sales. Susan has signed up for LinkedIn and Facebook. She's active in the local Chamber of Commerce and in her community. She has cultivated contacts within her industry association and knows peers at other firms. Mary, on the other hand, has not been focused on expanding her network of contacts beyond her immediate customers in the medical community. It should come as no surprise that Susan has many more people she can reach out to and get the word out about her job search.

In my referral coaching, I ask clients to think about how they found various professionals such as their doctor, lawyer, real estate agent, or CPA. Invariably, the vast majority came from a referral of some sort. Then I ask them how they got their current job. Most say they were introduced by someone they know. Then I get into purchase decisions regarding consumer items from cars to soap. What I've observed is that the higher the perceived value of the product, service or field of expertise, the more dependent we are on referrals.

Your vibe and the Law of Attraction

It's not just the magnitude of the signal you can put out that determines the power of who you know. It's also how you are perceived by those that know you—the "vibe" you put out.

The best-selling book, *The Secret,* reveals that the key to success lies in understanding the Law of Attraction: everything we now have in our life is because our thoughts have attracted it. Our "vibe" is our own personal signal tower to the universe and we are constantly sending out a signal. And, like a signal that bounces back to its source, whatever we put out there, we get back. This includes your career, your business, your possessions and especially your relationships. As hard as it is to accept, even the people in our lives causing us the most stress are often there because we have somehow attracted them to us. If you are open to accepting responsibility for how your choices and decisions got you to this point, there are pearls of wisdom just waiting to be found.

The bottom line of the law of attraction is that when it comes to being Referral Rich make sure your thoughts are focused on bringing the right people to you, not the wrong people. Ask yourself empowering questions to attract the right people into your network, such as, who is the person best able to offer me advice in this area? Or, who do I already know who might be able to guide me in the right direction? Or, who do I trust who might know someone in this field? These are the kinds of questions that get your brain putting out the right vibe so you can attract the people and circumstances to move you more rapidly to the achievement of your goals.

Referrals save us time

Have you ever needed a product or service and had to do all the research yourself? This is a time-intensive proposition at best and at worst might prove to be costly in the long run. When I am coaching advisors on how to get referrals, I ask them to explain why they think referral business is the best business. At the top of their list is time savings. Clients save time when they feel more confident in a potential new advisor relationship because they more readily provide the information and disclosures necessary to construct a successful investment plan. It's the same dynamic regardless of your industry.

The walking Rolodex

Have you ever met someone who seems to know everybody? Think about the most influential person in your community. It's likely they are a walking Rolodex™—if you need something, they know just whom you should call. Why not become one of those people others rely on as a referral source yourself? Here's a question for you: did they become successful because they know so many people? Or do they know so many people because they are successful? It's a bit like asking which came first, the chicken or the egg. The answer is both. For example, if you move to a new area and don't know anybody, it's vital that you begin getting to know as many influential people as possible as soon as possible. Over time, as you prove yourself in whatever capacity, whether it's as a good neighbor or as a savvy professional, you can be sure the number of people coming into your referral network will expand in a symbiotic and synergistic way. You will simultaneously become a referral source and a referral recipient. The trust you have in them and they have in you gets transferred over to others in need in a virtuous cycle of trust and service.

STEP #2: DEFINE THE BRAND THAT IS YOU

Regardless of who we are or what we do for a living, we are known for certain things. In fact, I'll go one step further and say that in reality, we are a living, breathing poster person for whatever product or service we or our employer provides. In many ways, we are a brand in and unto ourselves. That's why the best companies take such care in who they hire. For example, Fortune 500 companies like Proctor and Gamble, IBM and Coca-Cola are notorious for recruiting the best and the brightest right off college campuses every year based on the premise that their people and their brand are really inseparable. From the point of view of a referral source, everything we do or don't do is either helping our brand or hurting our brand.

The reason defining your personal brand is so important to boosting your referral power is our need for clarity about who people are and what they can do. Branding gives us an identity, which brings clarity in the minds of other people. Take a moment and think about somebody you know and admire besides family. What words would you use to describe that person? How did you first meet that person? What makes them special in your eyes? How did they earn your trust? How are they different from others you know? As you answer those questions, you will zero in on part of their branding.

Clarity

In my coaching work with financial advisors on their referral strategy, I teach them that getting referrals from clients is first about getting a clear picture in their own minds about who they are, what they can do and who they can best help. Then I guide them in how to get that picture into their clients' minds. It's really as simple as that. The more clarity they have in their own mind's eye, the more vivid that picture, the more success they will have in getting referrals. You can do this by going through this simple exercise.

First, sit down with the customers, clients or coworkers who know you best and ask them, "How would you describe what I do for you when talking with a friend, family member or business associate?"

Second, ask a sampling of these same people, "What three adjectives come to mind to describe me when talking with a friend, family member or business associate?"

Third, ask those same people, "Why do you do business with me?" or "Why did you hire me?"

This exercise will help you shape your messaging about who you are, what you do and how you can best help others.

Bull's eye

If you study the best marksmen, you learn that they aim at as small a target as possible for maximum accuracy. On a target range, this area is known as a Bull's Eye, the area of highest value, garnering the most points. It's the same when we are looking for referrals to help us get the help or expertise we need, or to help us build our clientele in business.

When you gain clarity about your own brand in the marketplace, you can begin to target the people you will need to help you or the clients you need to reach your business goals. How can you do that? For the purposes of illustration, let's assume you are in sales and you are looking to get more referrals from your existing customers or clients. In my work with financial advisors, I've observed that many actually have what I call "a natural market." That means that success leaves clues and, if you will take the time to analyze who you already have as clients, you can learn how to go find more like them. Remember the law of attraction. Assuming there is already somebody doing business with you, it's likely that you can glean enough insight from those existing relationships to help you successfully build your business.

7 ways to discover your natural target market

I'm sure by now you've caught on to how I like 7 steps, something I began after reading Steven Covey's *The Seven Habits of Highly Successful People* and have used in regular trainings and coaching. Right now, while we're still in Step 2 of the Referral Rich program, allow me to walk you through a seven-step exercise to help you determine your natural market.

Get out a piece of paper and a pen and think about one of your best customers or clients, someone you would consider "ideal." Do you have a picture in your mind? Now write his or her name at the top of the page. If you are in corporate sales, feel free to shape these questions to reflect the companies you are targeting. Below the name, write down a brief answer to each of these questions.

1. Favored demographics. What is this client's age, gender, marital status and family status? Are they married, divorced or widowed? Do they have kids or grandkids? Do they come from a big or small family? In my own business development efforts as a financial advisor, I found I did best with those who were older, the age of my parents. I also did well with widows. By contrast, where I recall struggling was with relatively younger executives. They were visibly uncomfortable when they realized how young I was. But the older clients had a different perception of young. If they were 65, then anybody under 40 was just "a young man." They seemed to not draw a distinction between 20-something or 30-something, whereas the 30- or 40-somethings often wanted the gray hair.

*2. **Common work status, profession, industry or business.*** Is your client actively employed or retired? What is their specific profession, industry or business? Examples here might be retired pilot, plumbing contractor or dentist. I recall figuring out that I did well with self-made entrepreneurs in various industries, ranging from construction to publishing. If you already have a background in a particular industry, this is a natural advantage. I knew an extraordinarily successful advisor who used to sell to eye surgeons and built his practice around this same niche. It might also be that you have a compelling narrative because of personal experience. For example, I've known advisors who did well with doctors because their fathers were MDs and they were empathetic to the needs of that group. Maybe you do well with other sales people or engineers. You can also use the flip side to this question to determine who you've had the worst experience with. There are personality types to fit everybody—it's just a matter of being observant and introspective enough to focus your energy on the right targets and simultaneously avoid the wrong targets.

*3. **What are their primary objectives?*** What was the specific problem that you helped them solve? What area of expertise did you showcase to earn the business? How much business have they given you in the past? How much do you anticipate getting in the future? If a client has given you a large amount of business already, it's likely you have demonstrated value to match that vote of confidence. If you are able to deliver that value to others in the same situation, you are well on your way to focusing your expertise where it is most appreciated. There may be multiple objectives, but try to focus on the key problem that you think had the most meaning in the mind of the client at the time. Every client has pain points. To the extent that you find those, it can give you ammo to take into conversations with similar prospects. Also, it's worth paying attention to what this client did not seem to care about. You may soon discover in your own market research that the demand for a particular service is not strong enough to warrant your time or attention. It may be far more profitable to focus on areas where there is confirmation of interest.

4. *How's your chemistry?* How did you meet this client or customer in the first place? How do you feel when you talk to this person? It's amazing how often this simple question is overlooked. Often we determine whether we like someone or not within seconds of meeting. This can even happen over the phone. This first impression seems to stay with us and actually is a very good indication of success in relationships of any kind. If you think back to the beginning of a successful relationship, you will find a gold mine of information regarding the relationship dynamic, especially that first encounter. Was this client referred to you? Did you land this client by cold-calling? Did you meet on the golf course? Perhaps at some kind of community event or trade association meeting?

How are you at reading people's reaction to you? Are you tuned into their body language? Do you recall how you were dressed when you met? How about what you talked about? Were you more formal or informal in your approach? Did you have data or information with you at the time of the first meeting? Did you meet in their office or did they come to yours? I've known many advisors who do quite well making old-fashioned house calls. These clients appreciate the "high touch" service of somebody willing to make the drive out to see them rather than making the client fight traffic.

How do you feel when you talk with this person? In my coaching work with advisors, I recommend using a "gut check" test to determine compatibility. The idea is to listen to your gut when you know you need to talk to this individual. Does your stress level shoot up when you hear, "Mr. Smith, line 1?" Life is too short to have it spent being stressed out with people you really don't care for if you can possibly avoid it. The reality is that we all only have a certain amount of "emotional energy" to expend on a daily basis. Some relationships are energizing, some draining. Imagine what would happen in your business or career if you could only work with others who actually give you energy?

5. *Similar lifestyle.* Any shared passions? What kind of lifestyle do they lead? What kind of neighborhood do they live in? What kind of car do they drive? (You can tell a lot with this one. Pick-up drivers are different from BMW drivers.) Where do they like to go on vacation? What are their hobbies? Are they active in any church or community groups? How about charities or causes? Do they have pets? Are they outdoor enthusiasts or concert-goers? What do they read? How do they dress? I've known many advisors who have turned their passion for golf into new business connections and referrals.

6. *What do you admire most about them?* Isn't it true that we do better with people we admire? That's because at every turn we are more patient, more respectful and more tolerant because we feel we are getting something back without really trying. Napoleon Hill once wrote:

> "If you tell me what gives a person the greatest feeling of importance, I'll tell you their whole philosophy about life."

This factor is greatly underestimated. Granted not everyone with whom you do business is going to be somebody you genuinely admire, but what if you could have that as a criteria in your business development efforts? Wouldn't that boost your passion and daily enthusiasm? Admiration also prompts us to focus on the positive in people. Surely there is something we can find to admire in every individual, and consequently we can set an example for others to follow.

7. *What do they like most about you?* What would happen if everyone you did business with genuinely liked and admired you? Wow, what a booster shot in and of itself! This question might be hard to answer but, if you don't know, take the time to ask your clients. It might be a character trait such as, "I know you are honest and will look after my interests." It might be directly related to your expertise: "I really like how you take the time to keep up with what is happening in my industry." It could be your service level: "I really appreciate how you go the extra mile when I need to get something done fast. . . ." It might even be that you remind them of a friend or family member. Whatever it might be, learn to identify it and you can have this in the front of your mind in your interactions with new prospects.

Take a bite of the Apple

One way to learn about shaping your brand is to look at how successful companies shape theirs. One that has earned a coveted place in the minds and hearts of consumers, particularly over the last several years, is Apple. Let's see if we can find clues from their success that might help you define your own brand.

I recently bought an Apple computer for the first time. I've been curious for years but had always stuck with using a Dell with Microsoft software. But the performance of Apple stock in recent years intrigued me. I began hearing stories from people about how they didn't just use their Apple computer, they "loved" their Apple computer. That's a pretty strong reaction about a pile of circuits, glass and information bytes. Then one day my wife came home with an iPhone, raving about what it could do. I had to have one! The mall parking lot was not especially full, but when I walked to the Apple store, I was amazed at the crowd. First I noticed a Starbucks across the way and thought, "Excellent store location." People would socialize at Starbucks then meander over to the Apple store to browse the latest and greatest in gadgetry. There was a buzz, a contagious energy that reached out, grabbed me and pulled me into the Apple world. This was more than a store; it was an experience. I saw others using iMac computers and felt compelled to take a test drive. I took home my first Apple like the proud father of a newborn child. I'm not yet a raving fan but I just might evolve into one over time. So what are some of the things we can learn here from Apple?

Innovation. There is always room at the top for the innovator—the one pushing the envelope, the one driving the next generation of products or services. When Apple came out with the new iPhone, it made a statement about their brand. There was nothing quite like it in the marketplace, and it enabled them to introduce their products to a whole new group of customers like me. Now, I have the iPhone, the iMac and will probably end up buying the next "iSomething." Steve Jobs, founder of Apple, has shown an uncanny ability to bring out new products that quickly become must-have items. I remember learning that Apple had a shortage of iPhones for their first Christmas season. This only fueled more demand. As you are developing your own brand messaging, ask yourself how you can push the envelope. Don't try to be like everyone else—be something new, fresh and unique in the marketplace.

Demonstrate value interactively. One of the things I learned when I walked into an Apple store for the first time is the hands-on nature of the experience. The whole layout is designed for interaction, and the customer is behind the steering wheel. I went to the phone and started pushing buttons and getting immediate feedback. There were knowledgeable professionals right there when I needed them. When I went to buy my iMac, one of the factors that sealed the deal was the one-on-one coaching on every aspect of using the machine. For me, that alone was worth the premium price. This is a differentiator and I noticed recently that Microsoft has announced plans to open stores. When I took my iMac out of the box, I noticed how elegant and functional the packaging was, right down to the way the keyboard fit into the bright white casing. I was so impressed with the packaging, I haven't had the heart to throw away the box! I've even taken my large screen computer from my office to my home, and the box is so sturdy and functional I'm confident it's the best way to move it. So it's built-in advertising—it's still sitting in my garage.

So how are you going about demonstrating your value in an interactive way? Are you offering workshops or a website experience that delivers a sample of what you can do? How's your packaging? Like a restaurant that serves great appetizers and gets you hungry for the entree, savvy marketers know how to get people to sample their service to demonstrate value.

Price is only an issue in the absence of perceived value. Have you ever walked into a business and wondered "why would anybody think they even needed that?" or "who would pay that price for that item?" But, if the item is selling, there is a market for it, pure and simple. Just because I don't like it doesn't mean there isn't somebody else who does, right? Different strokes for different folks. But make sure your brand delivers what you say it will deliver. Price is only an issue in the absence of perceived value. Apple commands a premium in the marketplace because they deliver something perceived as incrementally better than the competition. It's the user-friendly nature, the large HD computer, the visual appeal of the product. When I unloaded my iMac, it was so easy to connect, for a moment I felt like I had just hired a virtual assistant to help make what I'm doing easier. What is that worth? I felt like the product would be problem- and hassle-free because of the way my initial experience flowed. What is that kind of peace of mind worth?

So what are you doing to boost the perceived value of your products, your company or your services? If you want to make more money, the most straightforward solution is to find a way to add more value in whatever it is you do. The more value, the more money you can charge. And it's important to focus on helping others as the primary driver. If you ask for a higher price without adding commensurate value, you get the concept backwards. As Zig Ziglar said years ago:

> "You can get everything you want in life if you can just help enough other people get what they want."

STEP #3: OVERCOME YOUR SHYNESS ABOUT ASKING FOR REFERRALS

In my coaching work, I spend time exploring the anxiety most people feel whenever they ask for help, especially referrals. Once when I was delivering a training program on this subject to a group of financial advisors, I was cornered by a participant at the break. It seems that she had always been shy about asking for referrals because it made her feel uncomfortable, like she was looking for a handout. Then one day she got a phone call from a girlfriend in crisis. Her mother had recently developed Alzheimer's disease, her husband had been laid off from his job and their kids were going to need money for college within the next four years. The friend was in a panic and asked the advisor to help her. She sat down with her friend and her husband and consequently put together a comprehensive financial plan that would address each of the challenges. Afterwards, her friend made a statement that would change the advisor's mindset about referrals forever. She said, "You know, I'm certain there are other people just like us that you could help." Suddenly the light bulbs started going off in the advisor's head. Instead of thinking about referrals as being about her, she realized this was about *them*. She had just lifted a huge burden off the shoulders of this family. She began to change her attitude about the whole subject of referrals. Instead of trying to add clients, she was on a mission to help others in need. Seen in this new light and with my coaching help, she became energized and shed her shyness about referrals.

In order to overcome that shyness, we must first examine the root causes of it. So why are people so uncomfortable asking for referrals? In the highly acclaimed Automatic Referrals Jumpstart Program when I was at Horsesmouth LLC, we identified three basic causes of referral anxiety. As we go through them, ask yourself if you can relate to any or all of them.

1. Fear of offending the client. As one advisor said to us, "I've worked so hard to get this relationship where it is . . . I just don't want to ruin it." Referral expert Daryl Logullo calls it "the damage threshold," that imaginary cliff we think we're approaching, the line we're afraid of stepping over because, if we step over it, we're going down. We'll lose the client, or at the least do mortal damage to the relationship.

If you happen to be in any kind of sales, even when you're dealing with a loyal client of 20-plus years, you operate as though the damage threshold for the relationship is ZERO. In other words, if you so much as hiccup, you risk losing the client. Asking a client or a customer for a referral just carries too much risk, so we simply don't do it. Often, it's not even a conscious choice. We just engage in avoidance behavior and assume we're better off not even going there with the client.

2. Fear of humiliation. It's understandable to be afraid of looking unsuccessful or even desperate. Most of us have been taught early on that to be successful we must project an image of success—we work hard at it. We try to dress the part, drive the right car, live in the right neighborhood, belong to the right country club. We want clients and others to perceive us as somebody who's doing great and doesn't need any help. We want to look like we've got more business than we can handle already.

I've heard many variations on this theme in working with financial advisors. I've heard 25-plus year veterans say things like, "I'm afraid my clients will wonder why I'm asking at this point in my career."

3. Fear of looking "salesy" or "unprofessional." Nobody wants to be viewed as "just a salesperson." We don't want to walk into a room and feel that we are suddenly viewed as having a fin attached to our head as we hear the theme music to *Jaws* playing in the background—we are the shark in the water. Many people have this conceived notion that selling is bad, a demeaning thing to do. I have news for everyone—nothing happens in the business world until a sale is made. And we're not just talking about product here. Everyone is in sales to some degree. It may be selling yourself, your ideas or your value.

Some have a stereotype image of a "salesperson" as being a hand-shaking, back-slapping, always-in-your-face personality. We know there are people who just don't like to promote themselves by toot-ing their own horn. You may not relate to some of these feelings, but a surprisingly large number of folks, even in direct sales, do. They suffer from what we call "sales shame." And asking for referrals definitely falls into the category of "selling" in their minds. Like most things in life, shyness about asking for referrals is in our heads, a state of mind. And when we change the way we look at things, the things we look at change. Perception is reality.

Pain and pleasure

Another way to get your mind prepared to ask for referrals is by using the "pain-pleasure" principle. Anthony Robbins reminds us that, "The Secret of Success is learning how to use pain and pleasure instead of having pain and pleasure use you." This means you need to ask yourself a couple of powerful questions to get leverage by intensifying your emotions around getting referrals. Let's use some guided imagery to help here.

Start with the pain. What will happen if you don't ask for referrals? Make a detailed written list of all the consequences of not implementing a referral strategy. What happens to your practice, to your lifestyle, to your family if you don't bring in new clients or customers? Don't be afraid to get yourself uncomfortable here. What about all the people you could have helped but didn't? Imagine what will happen to them. We all remember the movie *It's a Wonderful Life* and the scene where George Bailey gets to see the world without him in it. Get a vivid mental picture of someone you didn't help because you were never introduced to them. See them struggling because they were never given the opportunity to enjoy the benefits of what you have to offer. Naturally, you want to avoid that pain. That's where the leverage comes into play, to drive you to focus on referrals to help those people.

Now feel the pleasure. Ask yourself, "How will I feel when . . ." and start to fill in the blank. Imagine having a record year in whatever you are doing. See yourself providing the vital help to the family, friends and colleagues of your best clients and customers. Picture yourself entering a room and seeing all your clients gathered and they suddenly erupt in spontaneous applause and begin to cheer when they see you. Then, one by one, they approach you with smiles and gratitude, even a few tears as they share with you how much you have meant to them and their family. Each of them shares a story of how, thanks to you, they are living the life they always dreamed of. They are better off because of your help and insight—you are a real-life hero in the eyes of your clients and your family.

3 keys to overcoming shyness about referrals

1. Become client centered. Most advisors, and most salespeople for that matter, don't think about referrals as being about the client. They think about referrals as being about building their practice. It's critical to embrace these basic truths:

Clients and customers care about helping their family, friends and colleagues. From the client's perspective, this is the core motivator in them giving you a referral.

It's also true that you have expertise and experience that can really help people. You can truly become a hero in the lives of those you serve. If you only remember one thing from this section let it be this: "A referral is about helping them, not yourself."

2. *Appreciate your value.* In my coaching work, I tell financial advisors that appreciating their own value starts with doing a role reversal, putting yourself in your client's shoes. I ask them to take a moment and think about a client within five to seven years of retirement who has kids they are putting through college and older parents they are helping to take care of. Think about what it means to them to have someone advise them on these critical issues. How important is it to prepare for retirement—to create an income stream you can't outlive—where there are really no second chances if you don't get it right? Where you are dealing with a lifetime of savings and sacrifice? How about what it means to know your children will get the education they need to compete in the future? Or to know that your aging parents will have enough to pay for their medical needs? How are you viewed from your client's perspective?

3. *Have a systematic process in place.* The last key to getting over any shyness associated with asking for referrals is having a systematic process. Having a contact management system is a must, as is being consistent. In all the research I've seen on referrals, there is a wide gap between the willingness to give referrals and the number of people who actually ask for referrals. Some studies show that as many as 90 percent of clients are willing to provide referrals but fewer than 10 percent are ever actually asked. So if you have a process in place that helps remind you to ask, you will ultimately be successful in getting referrals—you just have to ask. I've gotten into spirited debates with advisors on this subject. There are many who have told me that they believe if they just do a good enough job for clients, referrals will happen automatically. When I probe further and ask what kind of results they are getting, they usually end up bristling. If you don't ask, you don't get, regardless of how happy a client might be. I know a friend who put it to me this way: "You know, Bob, what has surprised me is that many of my best clients, the ones that are the happiest, have never given me a single referral." The bottom line is that we have to get comfortable asking, and having any kind of process to do that consistently is better than doing it randomly or just when you remember to do it.

STEP #4: NETWORK YOUR WEB: YOU KNOW A LOT MORE FOLKS THAN YOU THINK

Most people underestimate just how many people they know. I've read that the average person has over 200 people in their own personal network—professionals even more. Consider for a moment your own family connections and those of the people you already know. When I attended a recent family reunion, I discovered that I have a connection to over 12,000 people—just from one side of my family! Take a moment and consider the family connections of your existing clients, customers or business contacts:

Parents
Grandparents
In-laws
Children and grandchildren's in-laws
Siblings and their in-laws
Aunts, uncles and cousins
Family members' workplaces
Personal Rolodex

When it comes to personal connections beyond family, we often overlook groups like these:

Friends, local and distant
Neighbors
Social groups
Social and athletic clubs
Homeowners' associations
Landlords and tenants
Places of worship
CPAs

Lawyers
Doctors
Dentists
Architects
Alumni associations
Workplace

Take a look around you at work sometime and you might be amazed by just how many folks you know who already know you. Here are some examples to get you started:

Coworkers
Supervisors
Executives
Sales reps
Committee members
Board of directors
Human resources directors
Temporary workers
Assistants
Building management
Third-party relationships

There may be people in your world who are associated with your company or business such as these:

Customers and clients
Consultants
Suppliers
Contractors
Strategic partners
Real estate agents
Colleagues at other companies
Associations like trade groups or unions
Community connections

Have you ever really considered just how many people you know and who also know you in your own community? Here are some examples:

Local charities

Churches, synagogues, places of worship

Neighborhood associations

Local youth sports teams

PTAs and school boards

Local shop keepers

Local law enforcement

Fire department personnel

Post office workers

Community park visitors

Neighborhood restaurant and pub patrons

Think of these groups as being part of a larger network connected together to form a web. And it helps to write these webs out on a large white board or use a computer design tool if at all possible because sometimes it's actually seeing and drawing these out that stimulates the possibilities of potential new connections. For example, you might add a family member to your web only to realize they live in the same neighborhood as your doctor.

STEP #5: LISTEN WITH PURPOSE

Most of us are far too busy when we speak with our clients or customers to actually pick up on the clues they are constantly sending our way. One reason is that we are so busy thinking about what we are going to say next we miss out—big time. Often what we think of as idle chitchat can reveal extremely valuable insights if we just tune into what is coming our way. Don't expect the clues to be wearing a flashing neon sign either. Often the best clues are given in passing conversation. But if you learn to be alert, you just might have more opportunities than you ever even thought possible. This means we need to listen with purpose. What do I mean by that? Rather than necessarily ask for a referral in every conversation, what if you used a conversation to gather information? Then you can use that intelligence to methodically build a standing list of desired referrals for every contact you have in your existing network.

Let's say you want to find more doctors to prospect. You would ask questions like, "How's your health these days?" Note that many people like to share information about their latest ailment. This allows a conversational inquiry about what doctor they use or would recommend, which could lead to an introduction to their doctor.

The beauty of this approach is that you not only get to know new people to expand your network, you end up strengthening your existing client relationship because you are showing concern. Remember what we discussed about the power of empathy? This is where it can really come into play, and pay off. It also helps if you are clear about the kind of prospect you are looking for. Have you ever asked for a referral only to get a blank stare in response? This is because our brains work like a Google search—we need to have search parameters before we can find what we are looking for. It's the same when we ask for referrals. The more specific the better. It starts with getting a clear picture in your mind of the prospects you are looking for and understanding how you will help these people. Regardless of your industry or profession, the first step to any referral process is having as much clarity as possible about your ideal client—the people and situations you are best suited to help. Here's a good way to think about context:

> It never makes sense to try to be all things to all people.
> But you want to make sure you are all the right things to
> the right people.

In my coaching work with advisors, I ask them to idealize and think about the kinds of clients they like to work with and can best serve. Going back to the natural market exercise, the more clear you are about the kinds of relationships that come most naturally for you the better. It will not only require less energy and time, the ideal clients will actually give you energy. Think about your favorite client or customer. If everyone you worked with was like that, what would your day be like? Would your work become much more fun? Reflect back to our discussions about the law of attraction—that image you create in your mind will in fact be manifested over time. Those kinds of clients you think about most of the time will be drawn to you. The question is: Have you ever really spent the time necessary to accurately paint that picture? This is the most valuable time you will spend on any referral process because it lays the foundation for everything else. Like trying to build a structure without a blueprint, every client brick that gets laid may have to ultimately be removed if you are not guided by an overall vision and strategy.

Personality counts

Have you ever watched a really good interviewer like Larry King in action? He's able to be a bit of a detective without getting on the nerves of his guests as so many other TV personalities do. Whatever you think about Larry King, he's a fantastic listener, which accounts for his success. He once said the problem with most interviewers is that it quickly turns into an "I interview" where the person injects his own editorial comments rather than getting the real story from the guest. Let's say the subject is global warming. Instead of asking a question and being genuinely interested, an interviewer says, "You know I don't believe in global warming and I've seen pictures of the polar ice cap melting and I've researched the subject thoroughly and have concluded it's a crock. So what do you think?" It's no surprise that this kind of questioning is more designed to confront rather than inform. You'll get better intelligence if you focus more on listening than providing too much commentary with your questions.

And the winner is . . .

More to the point, have you noticed that most people in business are just not very good listeners? As we discussed earlier about the power of empathy, one of the most core human needs is to be understood. I'll give you a case in point. I was looking for a marketing company to help me with the launch of a business venture and it was fascinating to see how each firm approached a potential new client. Certainly, proven ability to do the work was important to me. But do you want to know the deciding factor for me? The short answer would be "chemistry" as we pointed out earlier in the book. But if I dig deeper, it came down to a simple question: Who gets me best? And as it turns out, there was a direct correlation between time spent with me initially and my perception of how well the firm or person in charge got me. If you are very, very skilled at what you do, it's likely you will get a certain amount of business eventually. But if you don't take the time to understand your customer's needs, you will ultimately lose that business to someone else who is willing to take the time to really listen.

You've heard the expression that "people don't care how much you know until they know how much you care." I'll go one step beyond—we all have to remember that from the first encounter, when we are gathering information from someone or about someone, we are demonstrating what it would be like to work with us. This means that we should make every step of our sales process an "audition" and recognize that every little impression adds up quickly. Do you want to dramatically increase your results? Be the one that takes the most time to listen, then do three things: follow up, follow up, follow up.

STEP #6: EXPAND YOUR SPHERE OF INFLUENCE

Thanks to technology there are more ways than ever to expand your sphere of influence. In this new era of blogs and social networking forums like Facebook and Twitter, the Internet continues to dramatically change the ways we can be heard. So what is one to do in this savvy multi-media age to have more impact on your intended audience? While the technology shapes the battlefield, there are core principles that will remain the same in the realm of human influence, regardless of the medium. Here are some of the basics:

Knowledge

Knowledge indeed is power when it comes to expanding influence and getting referrals. Simply put, the more you know, the greater their perception of your expertise, the more people will listen to what you have to say and consequently the more referrals you will get. Word of mouth is still the best form of advertising on the planet. So the question is what are you doing to expand your knowledge within your industry or to sharpen your skills to earn the respect that comes from additional knowledge? And perhaps more importantly, how are you communicating the message that you know what you're talking about with your clients and customers? Are you demonstrating your knowledge during each conversation? Are you asking questions that pave the way for you to display industry knowledge? What was the last book you read in your field?

If you had to choose between hiring one of two professionals—one who mentioned an industry conference or book they just finished on the subject and the other who didn't seem to be keeping their knowledge and skills up to date—which would you choose? We are all far more likely to refer somebody to a professional if we view that person as very knowledgeable.

Credentials and titles count

When you walk into a doctor's office, it's likely they will have a diploma prominently displayed on a wall somewhere. In fact, out of all professions, the position of doctor has perhaps the highest level of influence on people. It's ingrained in our culture to revere doctors. We greatly admire and respect what it takes to get through medical school and, when they walk in a room with that white overcoat, we're pretty much putty in their hands. Why? Because we associate the title of doctor with knowledge. We are confident that they are usually the smartest people in a room—whether they actually are or not is beside the point. They have great influence because of that perception.

In my coaching work, I'll ask, "When a client walks into your space, what do they see that conveys knowledge?" It amazes me how many financial advisors have plaques relating to sales contests won rather than conveying expertise valued by clients. Clients are far more impressed with certificates of advanced training and education than product volume. This is true even in traditional sales environments. Would you rather walk into a car salesperson's office and see they were salesperson of the month or certificates showing they have advanced knowledge of the cars they are selling?

My wife is a CPA, and I've always envied the level of respect that CPAs garner just by virtue of the title. They are like financial doctors who have no problem getting their clients to "drop 'em" and show it all. Here are some tips to show knowledge:

If you have diplomas, invest in high-quality frames to enhance the display of knowledge. Same thing for Continuing Ed certificates or other relevant training.

Clean up your office area. Is the area where you meet with clients or prospects clean and orderly or disorganized and scattered? It's hard to convey professionalism when your environment says something else.

Dress the part. When it comes to clothing, the key is to make sure you look the part. The more expensive the product or service the more your clothing choice matters. For guys there is an old saying, "clothes make the man." If you look the part you will be referred more frequently.

Grooming. Similar to the clothing aspect, make sure you pay attention to little things like your hair, fingernails, breath, body odor, etc. Nobody will tell you it's why you didn't get referred but, trust me, it's a factor in how you are perceived.

Give to get

There is a natural reaction that when we are given something of value, we like it. It makes an impression. Only when we sense that there are strings attached do we start to get defensive. The funny thing about strings is that when we look for them and don't find them, it actually makes us feel uncomfortable. This happened to me the other day when someone that was referred to me wanted to buy my lunch despite my repeated objections. I feel obligated to somehow repay him and I don't think I'll feel quite right until I do.

If you are a fan of the movie classic *The Godfather,* you know that the way the main character builds influence is by proactively looking for ways to do "favors" for people so that one day they will be in a position to return the favor. It seems that this is just a part of our nature. So the next logical conclusion is that if you want to expand your influence, look for ways to give. There is a law of cause and effect that says that whatever we give, we will ultimately get back.

This is especially true in the world of referrals. Do want to see your referral results go through the roof? Then go out and get new business or refer new clients to the person or company you are trying to establish a referral relationship with. Now, this may not develop overnight, but I can unequivocally guarantee you will eventually get results. There will be reciprocation and you will see that what goes around does come around, if you're patient. I've had people ask me how they can get in front of a big prospect and I suggest they brainstorm how they can do that person a favor. Figure out a solution for a problem they have and you will get in front of that person.

Endorsements and testimonials

It's no secret that sport stars like Peyton Manning, Lance Armstrong and LeBron James make as much or more from corporate sponsors than they do actually playing their sport. Why? Research has shown that we are much more likely to buy a product or service if somebody we admire or respect is associated with it. There is tremendous power in endorsements and testimonials. We all tend to live a bit vicariously through the experience of others. If someone attractive whom we like and respect says a product or service is good, we tend to believe it. And the higher our opinion of the person, the more weight of the endorsement or testimonial.

This is especially true for professional associations. Take a look at your tube of toothpaste and you'll likely find it endorsed by the American Dental Association. Or it could be AARP endorsing a long-term care insurance provider. Endorsements and testimonials are basically referrals that can be scaled up for wider impact. For example, if you see someone you admire on TV saying you should use the services of XYZ, there is really no need for that person to have an individual conversation with you.

It also helps if the person giving the endorsement is in a similar situation. We see this all the time on TV. The celebrity who was overweight but lost it using a special exercise machine or diet sends a message that "if I can do it, so can you." The lesson here is that if you want to ramp up your referral results, get the endorsement or testimonial of someone people respect and admire.

Centers of influence and leverage

Name any industry, any field or any community and you will find people who have tremendous reputations and garner extraordinary respect. This might be because of their position or title, or their known expertise, or something they accomplished or even because they just know so many people. These are people that hold so much sway that they are considered "centers of influence."

For example, in the financial services industry, CPAs are often coveted as a key source of referrals. They are often seen as an objective third party when it comes to investments and overall financial advice. Prominent attorneys or judges also can have this kind of status in people's minds.

The primary reason for focusing on these types of people is the leverage you achieve in establishing the relationship. Think about each center of influence as a separate broadcast television network. When you are able to get air time on their network, you can reach far more people than you ever could on your own. Having multiple centers of influence is like having multiple channels to communicate your message. And if you can get a center of influence to directly introduce you to a prospect, you will be in a power position to engage that prospect with the gravitas you need to get results.

Introductions

Many top professionals will tell you they will only take a referral that comes by way of an introduction. They know that an introduction can be the most powerful type of referral. Introductions can be done socially or in a business setting. They can happen in person or over the phone. In today's fast-paced world, we see more and more happening by email or on websites. But regardless of how it's done, make sure that the person doing the introduction is allowed to lay some groundwork for you. Like a farmer who tills the soil before planting the seed, you want the prospect to already want you before you actually make contact.

In general, going for an introduction gives the introducer the opportunity to tell the prospect what is unique about you. If you simply try to cold-call the prospect, even though you mention the name of your client, you will often end up sounding like everybody else over the phone.

Going for the introduction also gives your client the opportunity to discuss how they may have benefited from your work. It allows people to retain more ownership of the process that increased their commitment to helping you. This can be bigger than we realize. Think about it—they already know the prospect, so who is better at navigating all the nuances involved in securing you an opportunity to get in front of them, you or the person doing the introduction?

From your perspective, the introduction allows you the opportunity to save time. Can you think of a bigger time waster than to play phone tag because you don't know the best time to reach the prospect or you can't nail down a good appointment time and it keeps being rescheduled?

It also gets them to open up faster. You will be able to get more information in that first meeting when you are introduced so you can create a more compelling proposal. Have you ever had the experience where you sat down with a prospect and felt like you were just pulling teeth to get the information you needed? When they already have a sense of what you can do for them because of what they have been told, they come prepared to that first meeting.

Finally, you establish instant credibility. We talked about how good marketers establish instant credibility when a product is endorsed. This is especially effective when it comes from an authority figure, celebrity or somebody of high social status. We all feel more confident when we perceive that something is already proven to work by someone we trust.

As you think about getting more referrals by expanding your sphere of influence, the discussion would not be complete without asking about "when" and "how" to ask. Let's explore these critical factors in increasing your odds of referral success.

When to ask for a referral

Timing is everything, and it's certainly true in the world of referrals. Here are two key points related to improving the timing of your referral request:

1. When you hear clues in a conversation. As we've already discussed, it's critical to pay close attention during conversations, even during "small talk," because that's where you will likely find the gold. I remember once as a financial advisor being told by a client that he and his wife were moving to their mountain cabin full time and selling their Atlanta home. I found out later that they were selling out to a developer who was buying out all the houses in the neighborhood for a huge premium. Their neighbors were going to get a huge windfall, and I just missed, by a couple of weeks, an opportunity to be the first to reach out to those neighbors had I asked further about what was happening. Another clue is whenever anyone mentions the name of someone you would like to meet. Ask yourself: Are you paying attention during those casual conversations?

2. When you have just done someone a favor. As we mentioned earlier, you have to give to get. But you also have to know when someone is the most receptive to helping you. Often the best time is right after you have done someone a favor. I remember once in an ice storm having a tree crash right into the back of my house. Within a couple of hours, a truck pulled up and a man jumped out to ask me if I needed some help. Of course I said yes and asked him what he would charge. He gave me what I thought was a reasonable figure, I shook his hand, and after taking some photos for insurance purposes, he took out a chainsaw from the back of his truck and proceeded to solve my problem. When he was done, he told me, "You know, as I was driving through this neighborhood I saw a lot of down trees. I bet a lot of your neighbors could use my help too. Would you be willing to take a few minutes to introduce me to the ones we think could use my help the most? I'll drive us directly there in my truck." What else could I say but yes? And here's the beauty: when I drove up to my neighbors' homes I actually felt like I was doing them a favor, which I was. And he had a walking, talking testimonial along with him actually taking some ownership in the process. Because of his creative approach, he got all this inside intelligence that saved him time and made him money.

Once you think the timing is right, the next question is usually. . .

How to ask for a referral

I've never been big on exact scripting when it comes to asking because I think it has to come out naturally to fit your own unique style. It must also sound consistent with all your other communications or it will come off as stilted. In order to be most effective in your phraseology, find the right angle. So ask yourself this question: Does the person you are asking want to . . .

Feel powerful? Appeal to their ego—talk about how they are really the only one that can make this introduction.

Provide support to friends or family? I'm sure you have discovered in your experience that often there is sort of an "alpha" family member or an "alpha" person in a group of friends, male and female. These are the leaders who feel responsible for helping others. Appeal to that trait when you are asking.

Help others solve problems? There are some people who are just great problem solvers—they really enjoy the challenge or maybe they like to be the hero and "rescue" others.

Be true to their connector nature? Some people are just natural at bringing people together. They are very social-oriented—they like to introduce people to other people.

Help you because they're a raving fan? Some people get a charge out of seeing you succeed. You may remind them of themselves or their son or daughter and it genuinely gives them pleasure to help you. These folks can be worth their weight in gold.

If you are successful with when to ask and how you ask, you will begin to have success getting more and more referrals and building new relationships. But it's not enough to establish new relationships if you are not willing to maintain them.

STEP #7: NURTURE YOUR RELATIONSHIPS

If you had to boil down the one thing that makes all good relationships work, it is trust. If you don't have trust, you really don't have a relationship, or the ones you have are highly dysfunctional. Just like trying to grow a plant without water, relationships and referrals slowly fade away and die without proper care and maintenance. We all have to find ways to nurture our relationships if we want them to survive and thrive. We need to understand and appreciate all the dynamics involved in how other people are feeling about us at any given time. It's like we all have a trust meter. When we are feeling really good, the meter shows a full reading. But there are things we do that can cause a leak in the tank and result in a drop in the meter. So the question becomes: What impacts trust? How can we demonstrate integrity? Where are the leaks? Part of the answer lies in examining the key components of the science of . . .

Commitment and consistency

We talked earlier about how Dr. Cialdini in his book *Influence: The Psychology of Persuasion* outlines the psychological principle of "committment and consistency." Again, it essentially says that once people commit to a particular course of action, they feel compelled to do and feel things that are consistent with that course of action. The more they do to demonstrate commitment, the more driven they feel to remain committed.

Seen in this light, giving a referral or testimonial or endorsement has a profound effect on people. If they think enough of you to recommend you, that must mean you're really great. And through the very act of "going public" with those feelings and referring you, they actually create internal pressure to become even more loyal to you and to give you even more referrals.

You may have even noticed in your own experience that once a client does refer you they are more likely to refer you again and again. This phenomenon makes referrals a tremendously powerful way to develop any business or drive any cause because it not only gets you more customers more easily and more profitably, it also helps you keep your current clients and customers loyal. Referrals become a retention strategy, not just a new business development strategy.

The principle of commitment and consistency works both ways. If you make commitments and keep them you will strengthen your relationships. If you are consistent in your messaging and how you interact with people in your networks, you are much more likely to get more referrals. It really becomes a "virtuous cycle," where one good thing leads to another and another . . .

So what specifically can you do to demonstrate these qualities? Here are some practical tips to get you started.

Do what you say you are going to do. If you want to know where the rubber meets the road in building trust, it's simply to do what you say you are going to do. When you commit to something, make sure you complete the task. Have you ever heard somebody tell you they were going to do something and either didn't do it, forgot to do it or only partially did it? What happens? You lose confidence in that person to follow through on whatever they commit to next. And it won't be long before you will stop listening to this person altogether.

Do it when you say you are going to do it. Usually when you commit to something there is some sort of timeline or deadline. If you say it will be done by Tuesday and I get it Friday, the trust meter drops a notch.

Under-promise and over-deliver. It's vital that you control expectations in your nurturing efforts. That means it's better to under-promise and over-deliver. If you think it will get done by Wednesday, suggest it will probably be done by Thursday. Now, be careful here if something is time sensitive. Earlier we talked about the importance of speed so you don't want to lose the business because your turnaround time implies you are poky and behind in your work. But a properly placed surprise on the expectation front can be a big relationship-nurture boost.

Make and keep little promises. Be proactive about declaring small incremental steps about what you are going to do, then do it. From the moment you meet someone you are either building trust or tearing it down—there really is no middle ground here. And we must be proactive in our efforts. It's like a garden where, if you just sit back, weeds will pop up automatically. The weeds don't need any assistance, they just come in to destroy without effort on your part. So we all must be working the garden at all times to make sure our relationship plants are growing strong. We can do this by making and keeping small promises. For example, ask yourself, "What small steps can I take right now to show this person I will follow through?" It might be as simple as telling them you will call them at a certain time and then doing it. It might be delivering a work product at a certain time and then doing it.

Remind them what you just did. When you do something for somebody, try using the tag "as promised." This acts as a powerful subconscious message that you are consistent. And it reminds them of what you just did, which reinforces the perceived level of your commitment.

You've just absorbed a great deal of information that will help you become Referral Rich. Quick, which tip do you want to start on right now? Go do it.

8

Work Smarter, Live Better

Are you happy with your job? Can you see yourself five years from now doing what you are doing? Do you ever feel like your business is running you rather than you running it? Is your career choice allowing you to live the life you've always dreamed about? Has your personal life or health suffered because of your work life? Have you ever contemplated whether all the sacrifices you are making in your work life are actually worth it? Could there be a better way to do what you are doing? Is your current approach getting you the results you want?

Most people are living far below their potential and are in danger of waking up one day and realizing there was a better way all along. There is a way to live a happy, healthy, meaningful and more prosperous life in alignment with our true values. It's just that we can get so caught up in "making a living" that we forget to "make a life" in the process. As author Steven Covey puts it:

> "As you are climbing the ladder of success, make sure it's propped up against the right wall."

It's also true that we can accomplish far more than we realize at much greater speed than ever before. But we have to be armed with the right knowledge and wisdom to take advantage. And in this highly competitive, fast-paced world we all need an edge to be the best we can be. You are destined to live an extraordinary life if you are willing to open your mind and go to work on making it happen.

There are more tools and strategies available to help us be more productive than at any other time in human history. And there are ways that you can adjust your work life so it enhances not detracts from your personal life. In this chapter I will introduce some fresh new ways to approach your work and your life so you can truly work smarter and live better. Let's start with where you live . . .

GEOGRAPHY AND HAPPINESS

Where you choose to live can have a much broader and deeper impact on your work and personal life than you may realize. Have you ever contemplated packing up and relocating to another area? There are many reasons people choose to move, but there are some major trends that might make you consider a change in your geography now more than ever. Why might you make a move? In his book, *Life 2.0*, Rich Karlgaard alludes to shifts in key factors that favor folks moving to find their happiness: economic changes, technology, cost of living, spiritual needs, etc.

I've changed my geography a few times and I have to say it's been worth it every time. It really depends on the way you view change in general and the context of the move. When I went from my home state of Georgia to southern California, it was truly a culture shock. Why did I make the move? Well, I remember flying out of Atlanta on a cold rainy day in January, and when I landed in Orange County California it was bright, sunny and 75 degrees. I rented a car and took a drive down the Pacific Coast Highway. As I watched the waves crash over white sandy beaches, I could see in the distance the snow-capped mountains. Later, when I made a comment to my future boss about it he casually said, "Oh yeah, there are people who will surf in the morning and then go snow skiing in the afternoon." The ideal weather is intoxicating when you're not used to it. There was no humidity and no bugs. That night in Long Beach I had dinner overlooking the water and was offered a job. How could I say no?

When you consider a different location, it's likely you will entertain a different vocation as well . . .

THE ROAD LESS TRAVELED

In the investment world, it's usually true that following the herd will get you in trouble. In order to "buy low" and "sell high" one must be able to avoid the crowd. Some of the world's best investors are contrarians— they take a different path than most to find their success. It's the same if we want to work smarter and live better. We need to go down the road less traveled.

There are over 120 golf courses in the Palm Springs, Palm Desert area of southern California. And the busiest time of year is in the winter months when the snowbirds fly south from places like Minnesota, Canada and Washington State. If you are not a member of a country club, you can still find places to play but it will cost you a premium in prime season, from November to April. But my favorite time to play (though I confess to be a lousy golfer) is actually between early May and mid-June. The rates on the public courses drop dramatically and since the days are longer by then, it's possible to hit the links after work and get in a round before dark. And there are no crowds. It's a much less stressful way to play and the weather is still gorgeous. The real oppressive summer heat doesn't set in until late June, so I would play my golf during those "off" months with buddies who figured out the same thing. When you live in a resort town, you start to pick up on some of the secrets of timing and pricing. Over the years, I've noticed more and more folks making plans for when to do things and buy things based on various off-season strategies. If you try this, you will soon discover that you not only save a lot of time and money, sometimes you don't even give up anything of real value. Here are some examples of these strategies.

Restaurants

Happy hour food prices. We all pay a premium to eat at restaurants during "prime time." This would include Friday and Saturday nights. One of the finest restaurants in our area started offering Sunday night lobster specials at half price. If you are retired or have more control over your work schedule, you can take advantage of these offers and also avoid the crowds. You will often get better service because you are one of the few customers. Sometimes you can go to the same restaurant for early bird specials and save significantly as well.

Lunch menu. Have you taken a look at the lunch menu of some of your favorite restaurants? You will often find the same item at nearly half the price. If you like sushi or ethnic food, you can usually indulge in some of the more exotic dishes at big savings.

Food to go. Have you checked out whether some of your favorite restaurants offer curbside service or have a good to-go service? By avoiding drinks, perhaps some appetizers, coffee, dessert and a full service tip, you may gain huge savings in money and calories while you still get the food you like. And the bonus is you can enjoy your own bottle of wine without overpaying or without concern about drinking and driving.

Holidays and retailers

Shop out of season. We all pay a big price for instant gratification, especially in the world of retail. Buying that fall sweater in September or the Christmas decoration right after Thanksgiving will cost you. Get into the habit of thinking ahead enough so you can get maximum discounts. Savvy shoppers have known this for years but retailers have gotten much more sophisticated about the timing of sales, so watch out. It may pay to wait just a bit longer after a sale starts and watch for further markdowns.

Shop late morning or early afternoon. If you are looking for better service, try going into a retailer at off-peak hours to get a demonstration of a new product or to spend more time asking questions with sales people who are not trying to handle you and five others at the same time.

Check for outlets. Unless you absolutely have to have the most recently released designer styles, consider checking if there is an outlet mall within driving distance. These have become popular in recent years and offer tremendous savings on high-end items. Beware that the sizes and styles available might be limited and there are some slightly damaged goods offered by many. And again, it's better not to go to these outlet stores during holiday weekends or peak hours if possible. But for quality at good savings, they can be quite valuable.

Tourist traps

Avoid peak-season vacations. If you try to go snow skiing on New Year's Day in Vail or sailing off Nantucket Island in New England on July 4th, expect to get fleeced. Instead, consider alternative, offseason times to explore these beautiful spots.

Beware the three-day weekend. Have you ever been roped into going on a trip to a hot spot over a three-day holiday weekend such as Memorial Day, Labor Day or President's Day? Some may enjoy the mayhem but if you want to avoid the long lines, traffic and jacked up prices, consider going either the weekend before or after.

Traffic time

I've had long commutes and short commutes. A friend once told me that the best commute time was 15 to 20 minutes because it gives you time to transition from work mode to family mode. And when you walk in the door you have already decompressed from the stresses of the day. Short commutes can be seductive but insidious. I bought a house literally behind where I worked and, boy, was it convenient. But something happened over time I didn't expect. It became too easy and my world began to shrink—there was no need to venture out much. I became less social and more complacent. It was just too tempting to go home and lounge in my pool and hot tub.

Then there is the other extreme. I had an advisor in L.A. who commuted two hours each way in traffic. That is insanity. Even with satellite radio, an hour-plus commute each way can chip away at your quality of life more quickly that you might imagine. If you are in this situation and are not able to make a near-term job change, see if you can do some work remotely. Because of technology, more folks are able to reduce traffic time.

WHY YOU DON'T NEED HARVARD ANYMORE

With technology we can learn things with a click of the mouse that used to require years of formal education. It's not that we don't need higher education. To the contrary, we need much more of it. It's just that how education is delivered is changing rapidly. When I think about what it will cost to send my two kids to college, I wince. Given some of the deflationary pressures in the economy with the global recession, it's amazing how school tuition has remained so high. But I'm convinced this will have to change. Just as there was a stock market bubble and a real estate bubble, there is a college tuition bubble that will eventually burst. It's just gotten too out of balance. Even state schools that used to be more moderately priced are running $100, 000 plus for four years. At what price point does it actually make more sense to help Junior start a small business with the same money?

Or consider the amount of debt that many students take on to get their education. Aside from the obvious connections afforded the elite school graduates, what are our children really getting for their money? I'm reminded of the movie *Good Will Hunting* where Matt Damon plays a prodigal genius at mathematics who is afraid to enter the world of academia but instead solves a highly complex math problem on a chalkboard outside class while working as a school janitor. In one memorable scene, he dresses down a male Harvard student at a bar who is patronizing a friend trying to pick up a Harvard girl. He basically tells him that his Harvard education is useless and in the end he'll figure out that he could have gotten the same knowledge "from a $10 library card." Though the movie came out a number of years ago, that dialogue was somewhat prophetic. Technology is making the access to knowledge much more readily available than the library card he referred to. I heard recently that you can get MIT lectures now over the Internet. There are new innovative companies are offering "virtual classrooms" with "on-line curriculum" and "accredited on-line degrees." These educational innovations have begun to revolutionize the higher-learning experience by allowing students to earn degrees at a much lower cost while accruing less debt. They reflect new emerging realities about today's students who might be single moms or second career boomers.

While these alternatives may not replace traditional centers of higher education, it is clear that the Internet, which changed the brick and mortar business model, will also affect how education is delivered. Imagine being anywhere in the world earning an advanced degree—listening to lectures from the best and brightest over your laptop, while also making blog entries on your new online business website. Still, many cling to the traditional arguments about the virtues of the status quo. These include campus-life experience, and interaction with peers and professors. But the pendulum is beginning to swing. As we watch the world wide web and technological advances sweep and change every industry, keep an eye on higher education. The classroom and learning experience of the future is likely to look very different than it does today—and that's a good thing.

THE POWER OF RITUALS

When I was 21 starting my career as a financial advisor with no contacts and no real sales experience, I quickly realized that the only way to succeed was going to be massive, purposeful action within the framework of a highly disciplined set of routines. It started with physical mastery. Every morning before work, I would get up at 5:00 a.m. and run or go to the gym. This had the triple effect of sending a powerful message to my subconscious mind about being a disciplined person, building stamina, and feeling in control and accomplished at the beginning of each day. So for performance development, I recommend the use of a morning routine: "Begun right is half done."

Do you go to bed and get up at the same time each day? If not, you are sending your body and mind mixed signals. Are you getting enough rest? Regarding sleep, it's an eye opener to realize that our bodies will shut down and die sooner from a lack of sleep than from a lack of food or water. We must make quality sleep a priority, especially during challenging times. Sleep is when the body and mind recover, allowing us to wake up refreshed and ready to face the stresses of the day. And for those of you who are self-proclaimed night-owl workaholics, be warned. Studies show that mortality rates are much higher for those who try to get by on only four or five hours of rest each night. Consider how so many of the great industrial disasters of the past 20 years—Chernobyl, *Exxon Valdez*, Bhopal, Three Mile Island—occurred in the middle of the night. For the most part, those in charge had worked long hours and built up considerable sleep debt.

Have you experienced times where you felt unstoppable? Great performers throughout the ages have all described times where they could do no wrong, where their every move is effortless and flawless. They are "in the zone." While we know how it feels to be in the zone, the bigger question is this: Can we create that zone on demand? Imagine what would happen to your performance if you were able to instantly be in the right mindset and enter that inspired flow of serendipitous being. What if you had 100 percent certainty in your ability to create the results you want when you wanted them? Rituals can help you create your own zone.

When our football team went 15–0, it's amazing just how superstitious we all became as the fairy-tale season unfolded. We had a ritual of walking "through the pines" on a hill just beyond the end zone onto the field as part of our pre-game preparation. Prior to one midseason game, one of our star players was distracted by his parents who wanted to introduce him to a friend. When he started to go on a slightly different route toward the field, some of us noticed what was happening and shouted at him to start over and come down through the pines! Other routines that became superstitions included arm pads and sweatbands properly placed, having the same person help you put on your jersey, etc. We all know these are just psychological crutches, but over time they can actually enhance our performance if blended with practical exercises.

Think back to the last time you were really in the zone. To reproduce that same state of mind, ask yourself these questions:

- What exactly were you thinking and how were you feeling? (The more detailed the better.)

- How did you approach the problem, scenario or performance?

- Who, if anyone, was around you at the time? There are athletes who perform better when they know that a certain someone is watching.

- How did you prepare beforehand? What were your pre-game rituals?

- What were all the things you did leading up to the performance?

- What were you wearing? Believe it or not, how we think we look impacts performance. For many top performers, the costume, uniform or clothing choice results in a mindset change.

- What did you eat or drink just prior to entering the zone? What kind of sleep did you get the night before? There may be clues here if you pay attention.

Once you can identify all the things that were happening when you experienced being in the zone, you can take control of those variables to recreate those same results.

Repetition is the mother of learning

Many star performers will tell you that it's not practice that makes perfect, it's perfect practice that produces great performance. At the core of this is repetition. My college football coach was a master at the use of repetition as a learning tool. He used a "practice squad" to run the offensive plays and defensive schemes of the opposing team. The strategy behind it was that the more times we were forced to experience those plays, the more quickly we would recognize what was happening in the game. We would then be freed to simply execute or react with more familiarity and confidence. Our confidence grows the more times we experience things, so if you can set up those experiences in advance as many times as possible through repetition, you will more likely perform in the zone.

Our high school football coach believed so much in the power of routines that he insisted on running the same opening play every game. We knew what we were going to run and so did everyone else. And I think he wanted to make a statement of confidence with that move that was really intimidating to opponents.

Make the right thing to do the easy thing to do

In my coaching and consulting, I emphasize the importance of moving as many things from the conscious mind to the subconscious mind to free up mental capacity. In other words, the less you have to think about something the less energy is expended and the more you have to give throughout the day. This means we need to make the right thing to do the easy thing to do. Like brushing your teeth every morning, the best rituals are those that you do automatically, without thought.

Make a list of all the things you would like to do regularly but seem to require a lot of energy and discipline. Now, let's think about how you can make each of those activities as easy to do as possible. For example, let's say that you know you need to exercise more but you have been very inconsistent in your execution. Here are some steps you can take.

- Visualize the end results you want from the ritual. In the case of exercise, imagine what your body will look like, how fit you will be, etc.

- Make the commitment to exercise every day. People who try to exercise three days a week or some other arbitrary number have to spend time and energy wondering if today is an exercise day or not. There is nothing to think about if this is something you simply do every day.

- Do it at the same time every day. I like the first thing in the morning because very little thought is involved. When the alarm goes off it's time to exercise.

- Do it at the same place every time. There are folks who find this boring but frankly, that's the point. Is brushing your teeth boring?

Is driving to work boring? Is tying your shoes boring? Yes, you are more likely to do it when it becomes routine, a part of your life like eating breakfast.

- Do it for the same duration every time. Time blocking is where you decide in advance how long you will engage in an activity to the exclusion of other activities. This establishes a rhythm to your process and helps move things along effortlessly and mindlessly. You have it right when you actually forgot you did it.

- Reward yourself every time. This should be a small reward of relaxation time, a hot shower, a special snack or some other reinforcement for the behavior.

- Pay attention to what is working and not working—stay flexible to changing approach in order to maximize the results of routine.

You will find this process works on all kinds of daily rituals from exercise to reading to spiritual development. Some rituals are less frequent but you can apply the same guidelines for those you do weekly, monthly or annually. For example, you have a routine annual physical and you perform monthly or quarterly financial plan reviews.

Recovery rituals

Do you allow yourself periodic breaks during the day and throughout the year? It's best to keep these planned in advanced and timed to avoid drift and lost concentration. The most productive work usually happens in very disciplined bursts of energy, followed by recovery in a cycle repeating over and over. Just as a muscle needs rest after use, there must be a recovery ritual to get the full value of the exertion ritual. Many busy professionals discount this need for a recovery and face chronic fatigue and burnout as a result. What exactly qualifies as a recovery ritual? It can be a whole range of things, from lounging on the sofa to hiking on a nature trail. Notice that the recovery ritual doesn't have to imply you are sedentary. On the contrary, if you have mentally very demanding work, a nice strenuous wilderness adventure might be just the ticket.

TIME: THE ONE THING BILL GATES WOULD "GAMBLE" FOR MORE OF

Billionaire Bill Gates was once asked during an interview if he ever gambled at a casino. His reply fascinated me. He said the only way he would ever gamble at a casino is if he could wager money for time. In other words, he had all the money he would ever need or want but there was one thing he would gladly pay any price to get more of—time. If you think about it, time is a great equalizer. Gates has 24 hours in his day just like we do. There are 52 weeks and 12 months on his calendar just like ours. We could spend half this book talking about time management, but I want to share a few tips that I've developed over the years that can help you work smarter and live better.

Time can be broken down into snapshots. If I asked you the question "what is time?" how would you respond? Most people define time by a clock or a calendar. But those are simply the ways we attempt to measure time. At any given moment, there is something happening, and we can define that happening as a series of snapshots. Even when we think there is nothing happening, if we look closely there actually is something happening. We can break down and define anything as a series of snapshots frozen in time. This concept was demonstrated in the futuristic movie *The Final Cut* starring Robin Williams. The premise was that everyone had a camera built in to their own eyes at birth and entire lives could be recorded. Williams plays a director who produces a final synopsis after someone's death to summarize and celebrate their life.

Imagine your life as a feature-length film, and there is a movie camera recording everything you do, think or say. It captures it all. And the camera is always running. It is capturing all the moments. Try reaching out to an object right now. In order to accomplish that simple task there is a series of tasks that must occur—you must open your hand, move it forward, grasp the object, etc. It's within that series of moves that you can define what is happening. Your actions or inaction frame your daily life. When those snapshots are put together they become the film that is your life.

Control your movie, control your time

In order to better manage our time, we must learn to control the picture frames that become our own movie. We must be fully conscious of each moment in our lives, to be proactive about controlling the camera and what gets recorded.

Identify and prioritize

It's so basic and fundamental that many people know to do this and then guess what they do? They stop doing it! If you will simply identify what you need to do, broken down into individual actions, and then prioritize which actions to take first, second and third, you will be far more organized and productive than most people.

Utilize a consistent system

Any time-management system that is actually used regardless of bells and whistles is better than not using one at all. Many people get confused and think that having some kind of calendar is a real time-management system. Just as a computer is worthless without the operating system software, a time-management system requires having principles and a philosophy to operate most effectively. And it must be used consistently to get the full benefit.

SPEED CHANGES EVERYTHING

I remember being on the phone years ago with a client and needing him to send me some paperwork. He asked, "Do you guys have a fax machine yet?" At the time we did not and neither did many other people so I didn't feel too backwards. Of course, it wasn't long before the fax machine was a must-have tool for any business, and we were no exception. Looking back, it's amazing how many things that were so cutting edge at the time are now borderline obsolete. I can't remember the last time I actually faxed something to somebody. What did we do before cell phones or the Internet? I remember getting stock market information on an old machine called a quotron. We got breaking news on a device called a B Wire, which made a really loud noise as it spit out news headlines on paper. Today, there is arguably too much information and we need some kind of filter to separate the relevant from the irrelevant. The paradox is that while we are all more empowered with access to information, we are also more vulnerable to making mistakes based on how we choose to utilize that information. There is the need to balance information availability with effective utility. There is the need to balance ability to do something and the wisdom of doing it in the first place. There is the need to properly prioritize our values so that we feel good about the choices and decisions we make.

Case in point: the Internet allowed more people to manage their own investments and gave rise to a huge wave of "do it yourselfers." Online trading firms and their ads popped up everywhere, promising that the days of the full service broker were gone forever. They tried to convince the public that investing was easy, that the key to investment success was simply paying less in fees. Performance was less a matter of long-term patience and more a matter of chasing whatever was going up. The birth of "momentum investing" had arrived just in time for a fast-food culture looking for quick fixes and instant gratification. And if you had access to information and could trade your own stocks faster and more frequently at lower cost, you could do just as well or better than you could with outside help. This was a seductive line of reasoning and seemed to be working, at least until it stopped working. It reached a fever pitch during the dot-com boom when tales of smart folks abandoning their careers to become full-time day traders held out the promise of quick stock market riches.

Yet, fast forward 10 years and we find most of those discount firms either out of business, merged with banks or with radically different business models. Many of the same firms that claimed there was no need for advice are now embracing "advice for fee" as the only way to profitability. Everyone finally discovered that in a 24-hour world of cable television and Internet blogs, there is a greater need for advice and wisdom than ever. There is a yearning for having someone you can trust deliver that wisdom in a holistic way, factoring in our life goals and financial needs over the long haul.

POWER OF FOCUS: DO YOU SEE THAT PINK ELEPHANT OVER THERE?

I dare you to read that without picturing an actual pink elephant in your mind's eye. Let's conduct a little experiment. Take a moment and think about the color green. Now close your eyes and say the word "green" to yourself over and over. . . . Now open your eyes and look around. What do you see? What are your eyes drawn to? Invariably they are now focused on whatever in your environment is green. This is because our brains operate like a search engine and whatever we focus our attention on grows in our experience. We talked earlier about "the secret" and the law of attraction. Now I want to get more into the power of focus. This is so powerful that I will step out on a limb and tell you that if you only remember one thing about this entire book, it would be this:

> Whatever you place your focus on will grow, and whatever you ignore will shrink.

Have you heard the expression that bad things come in threes? Well, they can also come in fours and fives. But the good news is that good things can come in threes, fours, fives and even hundreds. It all depends on our focus. It's hard to accept this, but our mind really doesn't care where we place our attention. It doesn't place judgments on the merits of our thoughts; it just follows instructions. In that sense it's totally neutral.

Let's do another experiment to prove this point. Repeat to yourself the word "depressed" over and over. . . . Did you find yourself with less and less energy and joy each time you said it? Now try saying the word "happy" over and over. . . . Did you notice yourself having the urge to smile?

Sticks and stones and words

How is it that mere words can cause us to manifest the meaning in our reality? There are many theories about how this works but suffice it to say that it does work. Remember the expression we all learned as kids that "sticks and stones may break my bones but words will never hurt me?" We should update that nursery rhyme: words might not appear to hurt but they can pack a much more powerful punch than we realize. Our vocabulary and our internal dialogue determine our experience of the world. Words help us to interpret and rationalize our outer world. The broader our vocabulary, the broader our life experience.

My wife and I will occasionally get pulled into a reality TV show like *American Idol* or *The Bachelor* and I started noticing a trend. One of the most frequently spoken words coming out of the mouths of the various contestants was the word "amazing." Every other sentence was about how something was amazing or he or she was just amazing. Or the performance was amazing. Is that word really effectively describing the emotion or is there a way to expand on that? What other words might be more descriptive than "amazing?" How about one of the following: energizing, rip-roaring, joy-filled, bubbly? As you read those choices, can you detect the subtle yet distinct differences in describing a person or a performance? Why not enrich our lives by developing more nuanced ways to describe everything in our world and how we feel about it? When we are armed with better words, we can better manage our focus. We can better control our emotional state by having more choices in how we describe what we are going through.

It's also empowering to understand how words are used on us all the time in the media to arouse specific reactions and get our attention. For example, in the world of investing there are words designed to agitate. Have you ever noticed a commentator say something like "the market plunged today" only to find out it actually dropped 1 percent—hardly alarming in today's environment? Financial professionals learn early on to use "softening language" to keep investors calm, including innocuous terms such as "correction," "fluctuation" or "profit taking" to describe downward movement in a portfolio. There are words used to create urgency, warmth, trust, anger, envy, hunger, greed, fear, etc. You name it, there are marketers who have studied the impact and designed their messages accordingly.

Concentration

According to the dictionary, another definition of focus is "to concentrate." How long can you work continuously along the same path of thinking or work project? How susceptible are you to diversion or distraction? Can you deliver on a deadline? The ability to concentrate is a hallmark trait of highly successful people. I was watching the NCAA National Championship basketball game between North Carolina and Michigan State along with millions of eager viewers and I began to think about how in big-time sports every performer is totally exposed. In basketball, concentration is especially important when fans shake things while players are trying to concentrate. That North Carolina team was so poised and focused I got the impression that when a player was shooting, a grenade could explode at center court and they would still sink the basket—and probably go to the line for a free throw for being fouled during the shot. It helps if you identify and eliminate the enemies to your concentration so you can keep your focus and maintain your undaunted attitude.

STEALTH TIME AND ENERGY WASTERS

Have you ever gotten home from a busy day and wondered what you actually accomplished? Do you find yourself stressed and drained of energy but not exactly sure why? We've all experienced this state and the insidious effects it can have on our performance and results over time. If we want to work smarter we must take control of our environment by establishing boundaries and a radar that can detect even the stealthiest time or energy wasters.

In my performance coaching, I often ask people to do a self-administered "time and motion" study to analyze what is actually happening during their work day as opposed to what they think is happening. This takes some discipline to do accurately but it's vital to determine the "real reality." I ask them to divide up their workday into four distinct parts:

Early morning
Late morning

Early afternoon
Late afternoon

Individuals place their own time parameters to define the length of each section and commit to taking 5 to 10 minutes at the end of each period to record as best they can recall what happened during that time. To sharpen their radar, I ask them to pay particular attention to common potential time and energy drainers, such as TV viewing, Internet surfing, newspaper reading without purpose (more on this later), coffee or cigarette breaks, idle chitchat with coworkers, phone conversations with friends, socializing through text messaging, Facebook or Twitter, and many people's favorite—"organizing" your desk.

I also ask them to pay attention to negative emotions and self-talk that can sabotage even the best-laid plans before they have a chance to work. These include such negative loop questions as: "Why are they doing that?" "Why can't I do that?" "What's the use? The economy is down so it wouldn't work anyway."

I also ask them to identify people in their environment who seem to elevate stress levels. Relationships can either be energizing or draining depending on how you feel when you are together. If there is someone particularly troublesome, we need to find strategies to at least neutralize the impact. These might include avoidance, confrontation to clear the air, or interaction strategies based on different personality types. It's perfectly normal to have some elevated stress around bosses, key clients or customers, but most of that stress can be turned into energy if the right approach is taken. But if you find there is a consistent negative energy coming into your orbit and showing up on your internal radar, it's time to recognize it for what it is and do something about it. Here are some possible approaches.

Avoid. When I started out as an advisor, one particularly negative advisor colleague loved to spook rookies with stories of how few make it, how tough it is during bear markets and how clients are never satisfied. Those of us new to the business soon compared notes and devised a strategy to avoid his negative energy. Whenever he would come around, if we weren't on the phone already, we would quickly pick it up and start dialing. This actually served two purposes: first, we realized that he would not initiate conversation if he thought we were on the phone. Second, we needed to be making outgoing calls anyway so we found a way to turn his negative energy into a positive action. We even found ways to avoid being on the elevator with this guy. If we happened to step on when he was the only one on it, we would immediately exit, explaining that we had forgotten something at our desk and would catch the next elevator.

Confront. Have you ever believed something about someone only to later discover that you were misinterpreting some behavior incorrectly? Has someone just rubbed you the wrong way and you decided not to like that person? If you are in a work situation with a boss or coworker and avoidance is impossible, there may be no choice but to confront the person and/or issue head on. This does not have to be a high noon showdown. You may want to find a way to clear the air in an environment outside the usual work setting. For example, try asking the person to have lunch with you or go for a cup of coffee. At the right moment, just come out and say something like, "I've got the feeling there may be something I've said or done that bothers you. Is there something, or am I just imagining it?" Try to get them to open up. Often, it will prove to be a misunderstanding you both laugh about later. You might even become friends. Don't place high expectations on the encounter, just try to clear the air as best you can. In work and in business, we don't always choose who we are around or which people we get to deal with, but it's imperative that at least there be respect in the relationship. You may encounter a passive-aggressive personality type who will not be candid about what is really going on. But the fact that you are confronting the situation will likely give you your best shot at earning respect.

Neutralize. So, what if your attempts to avoid or confront fail and you still have to deal with this person's negativity? One tactic is to agree to some kind of "rules of engagement." This starts with recognizing this person's personality type and adapting your approach to minimize stress for both of you. For example, if you are extroverted and they are introverted, try toning it down when you interact. If this is someone who will be helping you with a project, ask them, "What's the best way for me to help you do your job?" Find out what process works best. Do they prefer communication by email or phone? Are they fast paced or steady in their speech patterns? Try mirroring their speed and manners to improve your approach. It's always a good idea to smile at this person as often as possible if you can be genuine about it. A smile really is a great neutralizer. It's awfully hard to be mad at someone who is saying they like and respect you with their body language. It's a boomerang that comes back at you in the form of cooperation and influence.

You may decide to only interact in settings where there are other people present. This allows an outlet so the focus doesn't have to stay on just you and the other person. In a worst-case scenario, let it serve as motivation to go for the promotion or have more input into whom you work with going forward.

SPEND MORE TIME DEVELOPING YOUR STRENGTHS

In chapter 4, we explored the importance of discovering and using your "pull." When we find things we are good at and enjoy, we have discovered a strength. And if we can learn to focus on our strengths, we will work smarter and live better. In fact, when you find people who spend the majority of their time working in their areas of strength, they will tell you it's really not work at all. Instead of draining energy, it actually produces energy. Like a perpetual motion machine, we begin to live in a virtuous cycle of serendipity. We are brimming with enthusiasm and confidence.

In the best-selling book, *Now, Discover Your Strengths,* authors Marcus Buckingham and Donald Clifton make a compelling case that we are all far better off spending our time cultivating our unique talents and strengths than laboring over and fretting about our weaknesses. So rather than simply believing we can reach a certain level of performance with enough hard work, we may consider how we would be better off spending our hard work on areas where we can make the biggest difference, impact and contribution. That will likely be in your areas of strength. I'll even go so far as to say we all have a moral imperative to develop our unique talents, even if that means keeping certain weaknesses.

Move weaknesses to neutral

As we all know, even when we do focus on our strengths, sometimes we don't have the luxury of accepting a weakness and moving on. Evolutionary forces demand that certain weaknesses get taken care of naturally. Can you imagine what would have happened to our ancient ancestors if a tribe member was not very good at hunting? Either he would starve to death or at the very least not be viewed as a suitable mate for the women in the tribe. In our modern culture, if you lack certain basic computer skills you are at a huge competitive disadvantage. Even if computer skills will never be a strength for you, it's vital that you find a way to move the weakness to "neutral."

Another example might be in the area of public speaking. Many studies show some people would rather "die" than deliver a speech. If you are required to make presentations and find you are not a natural, it's not the end of the world. But it will pay off big time if you can at least get your skills to a point where you don't totally blow it when you have to stand up and deliver. Of course, it is also a waste of time to put yourself out there as the one making more than the bare minimum of presentations. Instead, find ways to delegate that weakness.

Delegating a weakness

I saw a bumper sticker recently that caused me to smile. It said:

"So much to do, so few people to do it for me."

Are there tasks and functions you are doing that you can get somebody else to do? Is it likely that you would not only save yourself time but also get a better result? This can be the magic of delegating. Here are some questions to ask yourself to determine if it may be time to delegate:

- What is the most valuable use of my time right now?
- How much longer will it take for me to do it versus someone else?
- Do I have access to someone who is much better at this than me?
- Is there somebody else who would actually enjoy doing this?
- Can I afford to pay someone to do it and get the same end result?

Partner to compensate for a weakness

Have you noticed that many people actually marry people to compensate for a weakness? He's good at this while she's better at that. It makes perfect sense. In business it's common to see one partner better at the big picture stuff while the other is better at executing the day to day. Some are better at detail, the other at communication, and so on.

Partnering can also take the form of outsourcing. If you are weak in an area that your customers or clients demand, why not find strategic partners to compensate and make your offering even more robust? It can also save money. If you are a business owner, rather than increase staff, you can contract out for services that are not part of your core strength. Dell is a great assembler and marketer, not a chipmaker, so they partnered with Intel and made that a core part of their value proposition.

If you are an entrepreneur, look for weaknesses in other businesses as opportunities to fill gaps. Bill Gates famously outmaneuvered IBM executives by understanding how the operating software from Microsoft could be much more valuable than the computer hardware.

THE BENEFITS OF TEAMING

This is a subject near and dear to my heart. Have you ever thought about the power of putting together a "dream team?" Folks that find ways to make 1 + 1 = 3 create real leverage in business and in life. They can work smarter and live better because they recognize the value in letting each team member do what they do best.

In my work with advisor teams, I like to conduct personality tests to determine a fit for certain team roles. For example, if you place an introvert as your receptionist, you are just asking for trouble. Then I have each member take a personal inventory of tasks that they currently perform. They also indicate which tasks they identify as things they both enjoy and are good at, tasks they find energizing and most fulfilling. This same approach can be used to evaluate potential new team members.

Here are some "do's" when it comes to teaming:

- Do take the time necessary to do the proper "due diligence." It is far better to spend this time up front than to deal with the headaches on the back end.

- Do hire people with a similar work ethic. It is a major source of conflict on teams when there is a perceived difference in the effort being put forth from different team members.

- Do have a vision and a mission. Everyone on your team should be able to articulate a consistent vision and mission. It maximizes clarity of purpose and minimizes uncertainty and confusion.

- Do be clear on compensation expectations. This is a hot-button issue. There should be clarity about what determines and drives compensation.

- Do be clear on performance expectations. There should never be any doubt about how someone's performance is measured.

- Do provide "psychic income." Money is only one form of compensation. Don't underestimate things like fun, meaningful contribution, recognition, etc.

- Do have clear roles and responsibilities. People perform better when they have a sense of ownership of something. Make sure it's clear who is responsible for what and by when.

- Do have a career path. Many high-quality workers leave their current jobs because they don't see a future. If you want to hang on to good people, show them a clear career path and how you intend to help get them there.

- Do provide development opportunities. Make sure you are aware of individual development goals and look for opportunities to improve team member skills.

- Do have regular team meetings where everyone sees the vision and the results.

- Do have regular one-on-one meetings with each team member where there is a chance for them to own part of the agenda.

Here are some "don'ts" when it comes to teaming:

- Don't try to make a silk purse out of a sow's ear. That means don't put someone in a position where they are likely to fail. That's a colossal waste of time and energy.

- Don't send mixed messages. Be consistent when you are communicating to minimize the risk of one team member hearing one thing and others hearing something entirely different.

- Don't do all the talking. Are your meetings boring? It may be because you are doing all the talking. If you want to liven up meetings, let different team members set and deliver a meeting agenda. Make sure everyone comes to the meetings prepared to contribute.

- Don't keep your door closed. Do you have an open-door policy where people on your team feel comfortable approaching you when they have a need?

- Don't leave people hanging. If there is an open issue, make sure you get answers as soon as possible. It's very counter-productive to have team members worried about an issue that should be resolved quickly.

- Don't bring your personal life into the office. I know there are folks who just can't resist sharing their own non-work issues and problems. Just be careful because it can be a major distraction. If you are the leader, remember that every move you make is being watched and evaluated.

CAN YOU KILL TWO BIRDS WITH ONE STONE?

To round out this chapter, I want to talk for a minute about the role that efficiency plays in working smarter and living better. I'm sure you are aware of the saying "kill two birds with one stone," right? Can you imagine what must have happened at the moment that concept came on the scene? I bet there's some consultant with this original story of optimum efficiency mounted on a plaque somewhere. Here's a crack at what it must have been like.

A guy who happened to be a pretty good hunter was very hungry. So he went hunting for birds armed with a rock in hand. He spots one fly right down and perch on the limb of a tree. Our brave hunter takes aim but, right before he hurls the rock, another bird flies and lands right beside the first one. The hunter ponders this scenario for a moment then shouts silently to himself, "Eureka! What if I changed my trajectory just a tad and moved over to my right, released the stone so it struck the first one then ricocheted into the second?" Armed with this new strategy, he steps up and lets the stone fly, fatally wounding both birds at once. Ah, the tale around the campfire was surely one to remember that night.

Have you taken a step back from your daily routines and examined ways to do things faster, cheaper and with better results? This is what efficiency is all about. If you were to write an operating manual for your own personal productivity, what rules and guidelines would you apply? How would you measure your efficiency? Here are a few questions to help you discover ways to improve your operation:

- Are you using outdated equipment?
- Are you leveraging the Internet?
- Are you properly valuing your time?
- Are you paying attention to your total cost of ownership?

This last question is worth exploring. I had a wealthy client in the furniture business explain to me how many manufacturers had succumbed to cheaper materials and craftsmanship because consumers were less willing to pay for quality. He said the problem with the typical consumer is that they enjoy the buying experience far more than the owning experience. For example, let's compare the total cost of owner-ship for two sofas. If one sofa costs $1,000 and wears out in five years, it's annual cost of ownership is $200 per year. If another sofa of much higher quality costs $1500, many may conclude, "I can't afford that." But can they? Let's say that the $1500 sofa lasts 10 years, twice as long. The actual cost of ownership is less, at $150 per year. The buyer of the less expensive sofa thinks they are getting a good deal but, in reality, they will need to buy another sofa again in half the time. So next time you are in the market for an item, think through the actual total cost and how what might be more expensive in the short run might prove cheaper in the long run.

WORK LESS, MAKE MORE

I want to challenge conventional wisdom for just a moment on the sub-ject of productivity and number of hours worked. Just because someone works longer hours does not make them more productive. I have seen the opposite many times. Have you ever watched a dog chase his tail? He'll go round and round in a flurry of activity but he is of course only running in circles, getting nowhere. It can be the same with many indi-viduals and corporate cultures.

Here are 3 fundamental questions relating to productivity:

1. Are you effort-focused or results-focused?
2. Are you paid by time spent or projects completed?
3. Which has more reward: length of service, politics or performance?

If you are in a culture that values effort over results, hours worked over projects completed, or politics over performance, you are in a cul-ture that will ultimately lose out to competitors that take the opposite approach.

Many companies today are embracing:

Flexible work schedules, where employees get to decide what hours work best, when they want time off and how many hours they work.

Working remotely. As we pointed out earlier, technology is allowing workers to produce much of their work remotely from any location with an Internet connection and cell phone coverage. In the new global economy, knowledge workers will continue to lead the way as companies realize it takes fewer resources and infrastructure to support remote workers who don't have commutes or need office space. And tools like Web-Ex allow remote collaboration without polluting the environment.

Work-life balance. When was the last time your boss took time off or went on a vacation? Are you are in a situation where vacations are viewed as necessary evils? Do you feel guilty for taking off early to go to your kids' soccer match? There has been a backlash in our culture against the "work 'til you drop dead at your desk" mindset. I've seen people actually brag when they tell me, "I haven't taken a vacation in five years." They wear it like a badge of honor when it really is a badge of shame. How does your family feel about your workaholism? How's your marriage? Are you really living your values? Is it time to rethink your priorities? Are you at risk of career burnout? Many companies now offer childcare services as they begin to realize the huge contributions single parents can make if given the chance. And companies are finally recognizing the lost productivity from higher divorce rates.

Healthier is better. Enlightened employers are coming to realize that a healthy employee is far more energetic and productive. What good does it really do a company if they lose their people to heart attacks, diabetes and a whole assortment of stress-related illnesses? Nutrition classes, workout facilities and ergonomic work spaces will be much more prevalent in the future because they make more long-term business sense.

I'll go one step further. I think the companies that attract the best people going forward will offer work options with far fewer work hours allowing for much greater free time. The deal will go something like this: if you deliver XYZ results within this time frame, you own your schedule and how you do it. This means that top talent will not be constrained by the politics and the wasted-meetings era of the past nor the clock-watching culture of time spent at your desk, but instead will be judged on results and performance. This means real accountability at the individual level and team level.

Wouldn't you like to operate in work environments with priorities like that? Can you imagine how that might help unleash even more of your Inner Hero to achieve your optimum results?

9

You're On™: How to Start Your Undaunted Life Now

We've covered a lot of ground together and now, in this last chapter in our journey, I want to focus on the magical power of action: How to take control of our own destiny and actually make things happen day in and day out. That's the best part about living *The Undaunted Life* and making room for our Inner Hero. So, to strengthen those action muscles, we need to understand what they are and what makes them stronger or weaker. How can we get those action muscles to do all the heavy lifting required?

How can we unleash our Inner Hero and achieve our life's full potential? First, you must believe you are capable of pulling it off. You need to feel confident that whatever change may be swirling about, you can summon what you need to master your environment. Remember:

Change is a constant, control a choice.

HOW'S YOUR MOJO?

Everyone is capable of performing like a hero. But will your self-image allow it? If you do not see yourself as capable of stepping up to a higher standard, it's highly unlikely that you will rise to the occasion when you need to swing into action. Do you remember the Austin Powers movies starring Michael Meyers? In one of the sequels, Powers has his "mojo" stolen by Fat Bastard and consequently loses his ability to perform as a spy and all-around international man-of-mystery type.

So what is mojo anyway? It's courage. It's confidence. It's that sense of knowing what to do and when to do it. It's leadership. It's that swagger we all want, the spring in our step, that twinkle in our eyes that lets the world know we're going places. What does it look and feel like to have mojo? I want to paint a picture for you right now to properly set the stage for how this chapter brings together all the elements we've been talking about so that you can truly live an undaunted life.

SEEING THE LIGHT

Take a moment right now and imagine yourself standing in the middle of a pitch-black room. You can't see anything, you can't hear anything, you can't smell anything, and you are not able to touch or taste anything. You are in a sensory deprived environment. It's as if you are in deep space where there is just the sound and sensation of your own breathing. Your mission is to get out of that room but there is no visible sign marking the exit. No sound you can follow to the door. No wall you can lean against while you feel your way out. No signals in your environment to tell you whether or not one particular direction is more likely to get you closer to the door than another. The only thing you can rely on is your mind's eye, your heart and your gut instincts. You must have complete faith and trust that there is in fact a door—it's just a matter of finding it.

Then suddenly, you get a sensation that you've never felt before. You are overwhelmed with feelings of unbridled joy, unwavering confidence, certainty and conviction—a deep sense of knowing. A clear path is shown to you in a vision so illuminating that you are completely engulfed by the light. There is the door, plain as day. You feel so compelled to follow the path to the door, you are at peace with the decision to follow it. There is no need to resist the urge or question it. You are being pulled by a mysterious force inside you that you trust completely. You begin to move effortlessly as if being swept away in a beautiful current flowing naturally to a dream destination. You are oblivious to even the possibility of risk, danger or fear of any kind. There is no doubt. You are in the flow.

As you approach the door, you feel a surge of energy inside you that is explosive, you are now accelerating through the door, being propelled out of the darkness into the light. A burst of fresh air blows through your hair and it smells like a freshly-picked flower on a spring day. Everything you see is in vivid color, bright and beautiful. You feel the warmth of the sun gently over your face. You have a sense of purpose and mission. You are brimming with enthusiasm—missionary zeal. You feel in command of your future and your destiny. You feel more alive, more powerful than you've ever felt before. Your goals become obvious, your action steps intuitive. Moving forward with massive action now seems as natural to you as flying does to an eagle or swimming to a fish.

Now, I want you to capture that feeling you have right now and hold onto it as we discover how you can use all the teachings from this book as a catalyst to turn on your own life light switch—to move you out of your comfort zone. I want to challenge you to create a vision of your future that excites and energizes you.

CREATE A COMPELLING VISION OF YOUR FUTURE

Is there a part of your life or your career that is fuzzy and unclear? What do you really want your life to look like? Take a moment right now and visualize a picture that represents success for you in each of these vital areas.

Emotional state. What feelings do you most want to experience in your life: Joy? Bliss? Love? Happiness? Contentment? Fulfillment? Pride? Abundance? High energy? Satisfaction? Gratitude? Certainty? Confidence? Balance? Passion? Humor? Cheerfulness? Allow an image of yourself enjoying those emotions.

Mental state. What intellectual muscles do you most enjoy flexing? Curiosity, concentration, brainstorming, scientific exploration, analyzing data, observing patterns, innovating, maximizing, enhancing, challenging, developing? Allow an image of yourself experiencing these mental states.

Physical state. What would you look like if you were in ideal shape? Weight? Percentage of body fat? Clothing size? Blood pressure?

Cholesterol level? Breathing capacity? Stamina? Muscle strength? Cardiovascular fitness? Flexibility? Endurance? Allow an image of yourself in ideal physical condition.

Spiritual state. How is your spiritual life? Do you have a faith? What do you believe that can't be proven? What states come to mind when you think about your own spirituality: Hope? Faith? Unconditional love? Peace of mind? Pure bliss? At one with nature? In the presence of your creator? Connectedness with others? Giving back to the community? Making a difference in the lives of others? Picture what you are doing in the spiritual realm and feel the power.

Financial state. What is your net worth right now? What do you want it to be? What words best describe your ideal financial situation? Net worth of ___, debt level is ___, retirement assets are ___, investment portfolio is ____, real estate is worth ____, liquid cash is ___, college fund accounts are ____, my business is worth ____, my personal possessions are worth ____. Imagine what your statements would look like, what your properties would look like, etc.

Lifestyle. Now, ask yourself what is your ideal lifestyle? If you had the financial resources you just imagined, what would you do: Start a new business? Go on a cruise? Join a country club? Establish a charity? Retire? Change careers? Buy a new house or vacation home? Experience fine dining, culture, world travel? Imagine yourself in vivid color doing all the things you've always wanted to do.

Values and character. What kind of person do you aspire to be? What character traits do you want to possess? What do you want people to say about you after you are gone: Courageous? Integrity? Honest? Compassionate ? Empathetic? Strong willed? Trustworthy? Committed? Loyal? Faithful? Generous? Visionary? Leader? Honorable? Bold? Tenacious? Resilient? Dedicated? Fun loving? Optimistic? Intelligent? Charismatic? Imagine you are already the person you wish to be. What would that image look like?

The key with using visualization is making that image so compelling that it engages the subconscious mind to bring that vision into reality. It drives us to think about exactly how we can bring that picture to life.

GOALS BRING DREAMS INTO REALITY

Once you've created a compelling vision using primarily your right brain, you can focus on how to bring those dreams into reality using your left brain. You do this by setting and achieving goals. I know you've probably read about goals, but it's so fundamental to taking control of your situation that it must be addressed. And frankly, without understanding goals, we are doomed for failure.

Goal setting involves more than we realize. We are all goal-seeking organisms with a built-in guidance system. And, like a guided missile, we are literally designed to function best when we have a target. It's interesting to also note that having a goal does not mean you will get to your target in a straight line. Did you know that when an airplane is on autopilot it's actually off course most of the time? It simply makes adjustments to continually compensate. That means that the plane is usually going the wrong way but still reaches its destination. So it is with goals. We are usually moving in a zigzag pattern across the sky called life. And it can get pretty stressful when we don't feel like we are making progress. We can also feel stressed out if we allow ourselves to become overwhelmed by the size of a goal or by the sheer number of tasks required to achieve the goal. So how can we get peace of mind on our path toward goal achievement?

One drop at a time

If you are anxious about all the things you have to do—if you are feeling overwhelmed—here's a visual that can help. Picture a bottle of eye drops. Now get a picture of the end of the applicator where the opening is only as wide as a pin point. Sense eye drops are just that—drops. Only one drop at a time can squeeze through the tiny opening. No matter how hard you squeeze the bottle, the fluid will only come forth in the form of drops. It's true you can squeeze hard enough to force a rapid series of drops but they are still drops as opposed to a spray. It's all based on the design at the tip. It's the same with each task toward your goals. The reality is that as much as we think we are great multi-taskers, our brains can only actually process one conscious thought at a time. And just like that drop of fluid passing through the portal, we must become at peace with the idea that we are like that eye-drop bottle—only one task at a time.

Fear of failure

Winston Churchill, when asked once about the secret of success, replied:

> "Success is going from failure to failure without a loss of enthusiasm."

The major reason people don't set goals is that they are afraid of failure. If they never set goals, they can never be accused of not achieving them. The problem is that we have become a culture of perfectionists where we have lost touch with the importance of failure in the success process. Failure is fundamental to success in that when we fail we grow from the experience. This experience allows us to take a different approach the next time and repeat the process until we win through. If you show me someone without failures, I'll show you somebody who is not doing much. The most successful people are often the biggest failures. That's because they are in the arena. They are setting goals and sometimes falling short, but they are not afraid to fail because failure provides the necessary feedback to begin again using another approach, to learn from mistakes.

So where does this fear of failure come from? Often, it comes from childhood because of destructive criticism. Sometimes it comes from a learned helplessness that we discussed earlier. The beauty of goals is that it's like being the quarterback in a football game and having an unlimited playbook and an unlimited number of plays to try in order to score. You run the offense, you make the calls, you make the adjustments. And each first down is like a series of smaller goals leading you down the field, putting you in position to put points on the board. No matter how good a player you are, it's unrealistic that you are going to get in the end zone every time you call a play. You might even get sacked a few times. But by having a "balanced attack," sticking to an overall strategy and polishing your skills, you can improve your performance with each snap of the ball and ultimately win no matter the competition.

Fear of success

There are also people who are afraid of success. How could this be? Don't we all want to be successful? Maybe consciously, but what about subconsciously? What will your family, friends or colleagues think if you shine brighter than they do? Will they be envious or even sabotage your efforts? My observation among highly successful people is they became comfortable with success long before they experienced it, meaning they didn't set and achieve goals carrying any baggage about what they might lose when they ultimately succeeded. They developed positive associations with success and acquired an attitude of embracing the changes that might come with success. What do you associate with success? Are you concerned that family and friends might reject you if you become more successful than they are?

Money goals and values

When you think about money, what are some of the things that come to mind? There are positive associations like "contribution," "freedom," "financial independence," "choice," "influence," "abundance," "prosperity," etc. But there are also negative associations like "greed," "can't be rich and get into heaven," "the root of all evil," "makes life complicated," "my friends will treat me differently," "others will be envious of me," "people will want things from me," "it will draw too much attention to me," "wouldn't know what to do with it if I had it," "money changes people," "nobody gets rich without taking advantage of others," etc.

If we want to be financially successful, we must nurture the positive associations with money and stop feeding the negative associations. Otherwise, we will engage in self-limiting beliefs and self-sabotage, which will subvert our ability to earn the money or keep it once we've earned it. I saw a special recently about lottery winners. It seems that the vast majority of the big winners are actually worse off five years later than before they won the lottery! That's amazing if you stop and think about it. Here everyone dreams of one day hitting the lottery— we think that if only we could win the lottery everything would change in our lives. But there seems to be a paradox at work here. The people who tend to play the lottery are those least equipped to handle the actual winning of the lottery. They are not mentally, emotionally or spiritually ready for the changes that come with that kind of windfall. Some winners turn to drugs. Others go through divorce. Still others adopt lifestyles they can't afford.

Many people have a fuzzy understanding of exactly what "rich" means. They just know that after you become rich, you can do anything you want to do, right? Well, not so fast. If you want to be really humbled, go check out a yacht show sometime. I recall getting a chance to board a two-million-dollar yacht at a show and learning the tens of thousands of dollars involved just with insurance, storage and routine maintenance, much less actually taking it out for a ride. If we do the math we can quickly realize that, if interest rates are only at three percent, you would have to have millions of dollars sitting in a bank to make enough interest to even begin to support a lifestyle that involves this symbol of wealth.

What holds us back from setting and achieving our goals? What do we most need to move in the right direction?

Avoid procrastination. Do you tend to put things off? Are you guilty of paralysis by analysis? Do you let the perfect be the enemy of the good enough? If you say yes to any or all of these questions, you might suffer from procrastination. We've all done it. We set a goal and then somehow that spark of excitement never quite catches fire as we rationalize our way to inaction. This can be caused by a number of things, but the most common culprit is usually a variation of the fear of failure and rejection. As long as we don't do it, there is zero chance of failing. But it can take on seemingly innocent forms, so be careful. It can be a wolf in sheep's clothing. It starts out harmless enough with statements like, "I need more information before acting," or, "it would be foolish to rush in without better knowing the lay of the land," or, "if I just had more time,

I could get it just the way I want it." This approach can seduce us into thinking that it is better to wait than to act. But unless you are dealing with life-and-death issues where relative certainty is prudent, it's rarely better to wait than to act because:

It's not what you do, it's what you get done that really counts.

Develop a sense of urgency. One of the hallmarks of high achievers is the ability to develop a sense of urgency. When you do that, the death of procrastination is certain. How can we develop a sense of urgency? Picture an old-fashioned scale, the kind you see in a courtroom with the arm and two chains holding containers—not the kind you find in bathrooms. Then imagine one side loaded with all the excuses why you should wait to do something. Then imagine the other side loaded with reasons to move forward now. The idea is to remove as many of the excuses from the one side and add as many reasons as you can to the other side, until the reasons why you should move forward so far outweigh the excuses that you hear a loud thud from the falling weight.

I learned this lesson early on in sales. If you give people forever to think it over, they will take forever to think it over. I remember once prospecting an engineer who always seemed to welcome my phone call and enjoyed talking about investments. But he seemed far more skilled at putting me off than I was at getting the business. In those days, I kept track of my conversations on index cards and after a particularly lengthy conversation with no progress, I finally lost patience and confronted him about when we would finally do some business together. He candidly replied, "Oh, I usually follow investments for three or four years before I buy." My heart sank, but I learned a positive lesson. I realized that I was not giving my prospects compelling enough reasons to move forward. So I went back to all my current prospects that I had been talking to the longest and made a conscious, tactical decision. I was going to contact every one of them and, based on our discussions about what they needed, I was going to either close them or move on.

And as you might guess, a funny thing happened. Since I had been so patient up to this point, many sensed the sincerity in my urgency and to my astonishment moved ahead and committed to a course of action. Part of me was thinking, "What the heck took you so long?" And the answer to my own question was that it was me that had taken so long. Their delay had as much to do with my hesitation as it did with any other factor impacting their decision. Now some chose not to move forward. And you know what? It's highly likely they were never going to do business with me anyway. My results dramatically improved when I made the decision that now was the time. I did that by getting leverage on myself.

Get leverage. So how do we get leverage on ourselves to "do it now?" One technique is to imagine what will happen if you don't take the action. Get yourself into a state of psychological pain, the kind that drives you to want to relieve that pain. In the case of my prospecting, I knew if I did not improve my closing ability, I would not be around long enough to make the kind of difference in clients' lives that I knew I could make. Once you get yourself extremely uncomfortable with what will happen if you don't act, think about all you have to gain that will propel you forward. Use mental imagery here as much as possible. One trick is to visualize your various obstacles as being physically smaller in your mind's eye. Or you can even visualize a task happening very quickly. Let's say that you have wanted to paint a room in your house but you keep making one excuse after the other, and the primary excuse is the amount of time it will take. Get a motion picture of yourself painting but use your imagination to speed up the film so you are getting the project done in record time. Then force yourself to take that first initial step in the project to . . .

Run for daylight: how to create momentum. If you find yourself procrastinating for any reason, try to break things down into more bite-sized chunks. I recall my early days of cold-call prospecting where my goal was to speak with 40 people in a single day. This was such a big number that it became a de-motivator at times. So I came up with a way to play a mental game of small steps to create momentum. Basically, I committed to having my first 10 prospecting conversations first thing in the morning at the office before I did anything else. I soon discovered that when I had made those first 10, the rest of the day became much easier. In contrast, if I ever found myself struggling to make those first 10 calls, my day usually went downhill from there. It was the commitment to establish momentum that proved to carry the day.

After the initial 10, I would use lunchtime as an incentive. I would force myself to make 10 more contacts before having lunch. Only then would I actually enjoy my meal and would reward myself with a short walk afterwards. When I got back to my desk, I was now halfway towards my daily goal. After my next 10, I would reward myself with another short break and perhaps a snack. Then the last quarter stretch usually became quite easy. My skills were also warmed up and sharpened, and this was usually the time of day I would enjoy the most productive conversations. I was most relaxed and confident because I was closer to the goal line.

TIMING IS EVERYTHING, OR IS IT?

It's been said that timing is everything, but is it really? Are you putting off a dream because the timing isn't quite right? The irony is that my research into stories of success suggests that timing is far less important than the motivation behind a particular move. In other words, even if the timing is lousy, that timing factor can be totally trumped by the level of commitment to the new direction. And what appears to be bad timing can turn out to be extraordinary timing.

For example, let's say you decide to finally start that new business because you lost your job. And you lost your job because the industry you are in is overcrowded with competition—and the overall economy is down. This may appear like terrible timing on the surface, but is it really? It might just be the perfect time. It's not likely you will find work in the same industry anyway and, with the economy down, prospects for work outside your industry are diminished. We see this time and again where people in hindsight say things like, "Yeah, we thought it was bad timing, but actually it gave me the motivation to move forward with my plans, the ones I'd been procrastinating on for all those years because I always had an excuse. Now I'm out of excuses." And when you're living in an undaunted spirit, you can always make it "good" timing.

FORWARDS OR BACKWARDS?

One of the many success secrets I learned from my high school football coach was this:

> "In life we are either going forward or backward—there is
> no in between"

What he meant by that was that life is like a hill and we're on a bicycle. If we are not pedaling, gravity will pull us down. If we are in neutral, what we are really doing is going backwards. So when we think we are just coasting along, the reality is that we are losing ground.

What areas of your life have you been in neutral? Where have you been coasting? We can all find comfort in the fact that we are built to move forward. Think of our bodies as a car with no reverse. Everything is designed to get you where you want to go, not back to where you've already been. Have you ever bought the same piece of real estate twice? Would you go back in time not knowing what you now know? Successful people have a forward-thinking orientation. They are thinking about how they are going to get from point A to point B. They have this ability to see around the corner of life, to keep moving forward.

PERSISTENCE

One of the most inspiring stories about persistence comes from studying the life and struggles of Franklin Delano Roosevelt. If you look at how FDR battled polio with grit, determination and persistence, you can't help but feel all our troubles pale by comparison. We discover that all the roadblocks and demons he had to overcome actually served as the crucible to prepare him for the presidency. For example, in his early attempts to halt the progress of the disease, FDR endured deep tissue massages that were excruciatingly painful and actually made the condition worse. He experimented with countless treatments that all proved unsuccessful, yet found his voice by becoming a role model of inspiration for others afflicted with this insidious disease. And in those days, there was a stigma attached to the handicapped. They were kept away from mainstream society behind closed doors, hidden from the judgment and stares. The idea that someone with such a physical handicap could become president was truly unfathomable at that time.

FDR would go to great lengths to hide his handicap. He wore super heavy braces that had to be maneuvered with near impossible hip movements required with each makeshift step, to make it appear that he could actually walk. His speeches were very much staged events. One such moment occurred when he gave a speech at the Democratic Party convention standing up. That was all it took to convince some that maybe he had a shot at the big prize in spite of his condition. Such is the power of persistence.

"RUDY," "RUDY," "RUDY"

It probably comes as no surprise that one of my favorite movies is *Rudy*, starring Sean Austin as a pint-sized wannabe Notre Dame football player. It's a true story of how a diehard Notre Dame football fan endures incredible setbacks to fulfill his dream of playing for the Fighting Irish. He keeps getting knocked down time after time in his attempts to dress for a game. Once he finally got the coach to agree to let him dress for one game his senior year, that coach left. Then, when he had every reason to quit, when he knew he would not dress for the final game of his senior year, his teammates pressured the coach to let him dress. Those final 10 minutes of the movie are a real "gripper." How many of us would have given up after the first rejection? How many would quit after being a member of "the meat squad"—the group that goes against the "real players" who will play in the Saturday games? How many of us would suffer the humiliation of getting knocked down again and again?

The author of the famous book, *Think and Grow Rich*, Napoleon Hill, once said that:

"Persistence is to the quality of people as carbon is to steel."

What great things could you accomplish if you developed more persistence? How many times do you attempt to do something before you give up? Do you let obstacles stand in your way of getting what you really want from life? Do you "kill" your own best ideas before they even have a chance to get off the ground?

SHOT DOWN ON THE RUNWAY

If you study the history of what happened when the Japanese attacked Pearl Harbor in 1941, there were many brave pilots who tried to get in their airplanes to get in the fight. But most were shot down on the runway before they even got off the ground. It can be the same if you are too hard on yourself or if others express doubt at the beginning of any new direction or path in your life or business. It's during this incubation period that we must be careful not to shoot down our ideas before they even get off the ground. Like a seed that must be nurtured after planting, it's a good idea to not let the winds of fear or the flood of cynicism stop your growth just when things are starting to take root.

"WOULD YOU LIKE TO TEACH THIS CLASS?"

I have a confession to make. On occasion, I used to get in trouble in class for talking too much. (I'm sure that comes as a complete shock to you!) Many of us probably got in trouble for that, right? But did you ever have one of those teachers give you the line, "Would you like to teach the class?" The reason I got in trouble was that teachers learned early on not to ask that question of me because I could not resist accepting the offer! I was always more interested in the material when I had the opportunity to teach it. Suddenly, I was on the spot. It seemed to bring out my best. It can do the same for you.

Once I had a boss who did something I thought was pretty smart. He knew I was struggling a bit with some of my advisor recruiting efforts so he put me in charge of teaching the "best practices" around recruiting at a managers' meeting. It's amazing what happens to our self-image when we are placed in the role of teacher. It can be quite transformational in how we see ourselves and our own ability to accomplish something. Within a year I had a string of recruiting successes and was named to the prestigious Branch Manager's Advisory Council.

There are powerful psychological forces at work when we are asked to teach something to someone else. One such force is the shift that takes place when we feel we are doing something to help others. Let's face it, would it be worth going through medical school just so you could treat yourself when you get sick? That would not be a sufficient motivator to invest all the effort and sacrifice. Another force is that the preparation required to teach something requires going to a deeper level of understanding a subject. The spotlight will be on, so we want to be ready for whatever questions might come our way. It's also been said that a core motivator for people in any situation is to be respected. And that extends to respecting ourselves. When we become a teacher of something, we take on the role of the expert, the thought leader on the subject. If we are asked about our knowledge of a particular area, we can confidently reply, "I've taught others on the subject."

Are you looking for a way to become an expert at something fast? Dive right into the deep end of the pool and volunteer to "teach the class." It may turn out to be the best way for you to rapidly advance to a whole other level of expertise and success.

THIS IS IT: THERE ARE NO DRESS REHEARSALS

I love watching live performances of any kind, from stage to sports to politics. If you study peak performers, you quickly learn that they have been practicing, usually for many years to perfect their craft. But in life, it's important that we don't view our day-to-day routine as a mere warm-up or a practice round. The fact is that this is it. Every day we are "on stage," so it's important that we make it count. I think one of the reasons many people perform far below their potential is that they don't fully appreciate the fact that our time on this earth is very short in the big scheme of things. And if we look at our lives like a live performance, we begin to realize that there are no dress rehearsals. One way to think about your life is to pretend that it is being filmed. What if you were on camera all the time? What if every action you took, everything you said, was recorded for all eternity? And you would be judged by later generations for how well you spent your time here on earth?

WHAT WILL YOUR MARK BE?

At the end of your days looking back, what do you want to have stood for? What do you want engraved on your tombstone? What do you want to have said about you? Take a moment right now and think about your legacy—your mark. Here is a list to get you thinking about it:

Inspired	Achiever
Courageous	Confident
Faithful	Strong
Determined	Healthy
Powerful	Generous
Influential	Talented
Integrity in all things	Disciplined
Loving	Dedicated
Compassionate	Devoted
Honest	Visionary
Playful	Creative
Passionate	Giving
Grateful	Committed
Explorer	Loyal
Leader	Knowledgeable
Cheerful	Insightful
Optimist	Worthy
Energized	Respected
Wealthy	Balanced
Prosperous	Strategic
Happy	Engaged
Joyful	Resilient
Enthusiastic	Empathetic
Fun loving	Decisive

Action oriented	Patient
Results driven	Honorable
Curious	Compelling
Flexible	Ambitious
Appreciative	Explosive
Invested	Bold
Contributor	Audacious
Unstoppable	Innovative
Hopeful	Wise
Responsible	Spiritual
Tenacious	Selfless

You may want to choose a Top 10 or Top 5 list of traits you most want to guide you as you pursue your Undaunted Life. As you move your Inner Hero more to the center of your stage, feel free to also draw inspiration from the heroes you see in daily life. Remember the Miracle on the Hudson and how that pilot, Sully Sullenberger, had to react in a totally undaunted way to land that plane? The moment he realized that there had been a bird strike in the engines, he recognized what he was going to have to do to make sure that 155 people all had the best chance of survival. Then he utilized his vast knowledge and experience to execute that amazing water landing. "All of my years of training and experience was really preparing me for a moment like this," he said.

And he was ready. You can be too—ready for each and every moment to be your best at whatever you do. No matter what.

"CREW WANTED FOR HARSH JOURNEY: SMALL WAGES, BITTER COLD, SAFE RETURN DOUBTFUL"

I want to close with one of my all-time favorite stories. The above caption was an actual ad placed in a newspaper in 1914 by Sir Ernest Shackleton, a famous British explorer. He was putting together an expedition to become the first to hike across the continent of Antarctica. The story of his expedition can teach us a lot about courage, leadership and truly living *The Undaunted Life—to succeed no matter what.*

Imagine for a moment that you are on this expedition with Shackleton.

In 1914, Shackleton the explorer became Shackleton the recruiter. When he placed that ad looking for a crew, over 5,000 responded. He then hand-picked a select crew of 27, the cream of the crop, to be on his team. He knew that his success would come down to the quality of his people and the trust they placed in him, in themselves and in each other.

He also knew they needed the right equipment, tools and supplies, which started with the right kind of boat. He purchased a specially-made ship for the journey. It was built of oak and Norwegian fir. Some of the planks were two and a half feet thick. She was meticulously designed to withstand the ice. She was called *The Endurance.*

In August 1914, he sailed south. Then, when he came within less than 100 miles from the Antarctic shore, the temperature suddenly dropped from 20 degrees above zero to 20 degrees below zero. And his ship became trapped in the ice of the frozen ocean.

At this point Shackleton's true greatness as a leader came to the surface. Without a moment's hesitation he changed the focus of his expedition from trekking across Antarctica to simply getting his men back alive. Witnesses say that he showed no rage or disappointment but simply said, "We must prepare for winter," and then went to work. And what a winter it was—after three months where the days were as dark as the nights, huge blocks of ice started buckling against the ship. And the timbers of the ship began to crack. The sound was like firecrackers going off on the Fourth of July.

Then, as if they didn't have enough problems, a blizzard hit. One of his officers, an Irishman, whispered to Shackleton these haunting words: "The ship, Sir. . . . you know it's only a matter of time . . . what the ice gets, the ice keeps."

But Shackleton showed no fear. Instead, during the worst of the blizzard, he worked harder than anyone on that crew. In fact, he didn't lie down for three days—he didn't change clothes for 10 days.

After months of being trapped in the ice, Shackleton finally gave the order to abandon ship. They unloaded what supplies they could, including three lifeboats, some tents and sleeping bags.

The first night was 15 degrees below zero. And not all the sleeping bags had fur so they had a drawing to see who would get them. Shackleton and his officers rigged the drawing so that all the fur bags went to the crew members under them.

Food was scarce—each man was rationed one sea biscuit per day. One crew member described it this way: "We looked at our biscuit for breakfast, sucked on it for lunch and ate it for dinner."

They boarded their lifeboats and rowed day after day looking for land until finally they ran into an island, only to realize if was not on anybody's sea route. So Shackleton made a risky bet. He would take six crew members in one of the lifeboats and attempt to sail 800 miles across the most dangerous ocean in the world to reach South Georgia Island. They left 21 men behind to hang on until a rescue could be arranged.

To navigate, they needed the sun and the horizon, but often they could see neither. They relied on an experienced navigator who used a crude navigation tool. He knew that every one-degree miscalculation meant drifting 60 miles off course.

Then, amazingly, on May 10, 1906, they made it to South Georgia Island. Ultimately, the entire crew was rescued.

The most miraculous part of this story is that despite incredible hardship and struggle, not a single life had been lost.

The name Shackleton gave his ship, *The Endurance*, was based on his family motto: By Endurance We Conquer.

As you face the inevitable challenges of life, remember that the cornerstone of Shackleton's character was his dogged optimism. And by leading *The Undaunted Life,* you can conquer too.

ABOUT THE AUTHOR

Bob David is a professional speaker, success coach and business consultant. After more than 20 years of learning, executing and teaching success strategies, he founded Bob David Live Inc. to inspire, entertain, educate, coach and advise people in ways that maximize their potential, performance and happiness—to lead them on a journey of personal and professional development, purposeful contribution, financial success and life long goal achievement. And to help them have much more fun and laughs along the way.

Learn more about Bob's services at:
   www.bobdavidlive.com
   and
   www.bobasbill.com

Breinigsville, PA USA
13 October 2010
247315BV00004B/77/P